W9-BXX-769

LEBRON
JAMES
★ ★ ★ ★ ★ VS. ★ ★ ★ ★ ★ ★
THE NBA

LEBRON
JAMES
★ ★ ★ ★ ★ ★ ★ **VS.** ★ ★ ★ ★ ★ ★ ★ ★
THE NBA

BRENDAN BOWERS

TRIUMPH
B O O K S

Copyright © 2017 by Brendan Bowers

No part of this publication may be reproduced, stored in a retrieval system, or transmitted in any form by any means, electronic, mechanical, photocopying, or otherwise, without the prior written permission of the publisher, Triumph Books LLC, 814 North Franklin Street, Chicago, Illinois 60610.

Library of Congress Cataloging-in-Publication Data available upon request.

This book is available in quantity at special discounts for your group or organization. For further information, contact:

Triumph Books LLC
814 North Franklin Street
Chicago, Illinois 60610
(312) 337-0747
www.triumphbooks.com

Printed in U.S.A.
ISBN: 978-1-62937-440-6
Design by Patricia Frey
Page production by Nord Compo
All photos are courtesy of AP Images except where otherwise noted.

In the 1980s, Cleveland Browns coach Sam Rutigliano teamed up with Dr. Gregory Collins to create the Inner Circle Foundation. The program was dedicated to helping Browns players improve mental health and maintain drug-free lifestyles. Their model now serves as the template for all NFL teams.

Today, Coach Sam's Inner Circle Foundation has expanded to provide educational support to at-risk children in the third grade. The foundation offers a combination of literacy, personal development, and health programs throughout several public elementary schools in Cleveland, Ohio.

Recently, I was blessed to become a reading tutor for Coach Sam's at Robert H. Jamison School. Witnessing the overwhelming passion for literacy from both students and teachers has been inspiring. This book is dedicated to raising awareness for that mission. For more on Coach Sam's Inner Circle Foundation visit: http://innercirclefoundation.org/

Finally, special thanks to my mom and dad, John and Eileen Bowers; brothers, Kevin and Trevor; and love of my life, Kate.

★ ★ ★
Contents

★ ★ ★

Foreword

I'm not sure what sort of first impression the average 16-year-old kid can be expected to make. I only know now what I suspected then: that LeBron James was no average 16-year-old.

It was the spring of 2001, late in his sophomore year of high school, when I traveled from New York to Akron, Ohio, to meet the kid who had the basketball world buzzing. He wasn't yet famous, at least not among the general public—that would come soon enough—but for those of us who paid attention to high school basketball, his unique name was one we'd been hearing for a while. By that time, he was already a two-time state champion, and that season he'd been named Ohio's Mr. Basketball; not long before my visit, *USA Today* named him a first-team All-American. These were the sorts of accolades that justified a national magazine sending a writer to spend a few days in Akron.

And that first impression? I met him first in the lunchroom at St. Vincent-St. Mary High School, just up the hill from downtown Akron. I liked him immediately. He was funny, a fast talker and obvious leader in his group of teammates and friends, massively confident even as he had yet to fully grow into his then 6'6" frame. Over the next couple of years, that impression would be reconfirmed again and again: the sense of humor, the knack for knowing every word to seemingly every rap song he heard, the innate leadership skills that showed themselves on and off the court. He was an easy kid to like. And all of this was without a basketball in his hands.

If anything, I was less sure of my impression of him *on* the court; I might be the only person alive who came away underwhelmed the first time I saw him play. In fairness, it wasn't an actual game, just a postseason pickup run with teammates at the St. V gym. His physical gifts—size, speed, athleticism, explosiveness—were obvious, but his play was sloppy, and he looked disinterested. On natural ability alone, it was easy to see that he was a great high school basketball player. But beyond that? If this was all I had to go on, how impressed could I be?

I've never been one for predictions, but almost inevitably where a teenage basketball phenom is concerned, the first thing that anyone asks is: *How good can he be?* In covering him through his next two years of summer and high school basketball, it was a question I asked—and *was* asked—often. (For what it's worth, I thought he'd be a multi-time NBA All-Star, a guy who averaged 20-some points a game and regularly flirted with triple-doubles, but perhaps not the dominant force he became.) But the answer that always stuck with me came from Keith Dambrot, the man who coached him his first two seasons at St. V, and a man who had every reason to try to downplay the hype swirling around his young star.

Instead, Dambrot answered with an honesty that only fueled the buzz: He thought LeBron was the best high school player in the state as a freshman, and that he was probably the best player in the country as a sophomore. Looking into the future, and to LeBron's professional prospects, the coach was matter of fact: He saw no reason why LeBron couldn't be an all-time great.

At the time, the prediction seemed optimistic, if not a little bit reckless. As we've known for years now, it was entirely accurate.

★ ★ ★

There's an almost automatic follow-up to that question, of course: It's not only "How good can he be?" but "Can he be better than _____?" It's a question that's been swirling around LeBron since high school, and again, it's one Dambrot answered as convincingly as anyone. Even then, way back in 2001, the coach saw his sophomore star as a hybrid of Tracy McGrady, Kobe Bryant, and Magic Johnson. It was a staggering comparison, and while Dambrot wasn't claiming this 16-year-old was on their level just yet, the coach fully believed LeBron could be, and *would* be, if he wanted it badly enough.

Again, we now know how that turned out. He's not yet done playing, and even if he was, there's no definitive way to determine where LeBron ranks among such all-time greats, let alone Michael Jordan, the player he grew up idolizing and the closest thing to a consensus best-ever the League has seen. But with 14 seasons, almost 29,000 career points, four MVP awards, and three NBA titles under LeBron's belt as I write this, it hardly seems too early to consider his legacy.

With that in mind, I was immediately intrigued when Brendan explained the concept for this book. Sporting legacies don't *have* to extend beyond the boundaries of the competitor's court or field, but the best of them—Muhammad Ali, Jackie Robinson, Bill Russell, and Billie Jean King come immediately to mind—are directly tied to what they accomplished beyond the box score. You can debate whether LeBron belongs in such company, but in a different era, under very different circumstances, he has built an on-and-off-court legacy that dwarfs that of his peers.

His social stances might not be as risky as they were for the legends mentioned above, but they carry risk nonetheless, and he's grown into them naturally. He's done so even as he's built a broad business empire with interests in everything from fast food to Hollywood, proving himself a savvy businessman with sharp instincts. Most impressively, he's used the weight of his wealth and fame to lift up his community, partnering with Akron-based businesses, local government, and even his hometown university to encourage healthier lifestyles and guarantee a college education for thousands of kids.

It's crazy to think of all this now in the context of that first impression, way back in the spring of 2001, the tall, quick-witted kid trading jokes with his buddies about whose sneakers were in worse shape, who teased me after I'd grown out my beard for "looking like Jesus," or who, at dinner for an interview a year later, put away two root beer floats before his food arrived. He was a kid, a talented and engaging one with sky-high potential, but a kid nonetheless. He's grown into a CEO, a husband and father with kids as old as my own, a social activist and community hero, and one of the greatest basketball players of all time.

With all this in mind, I'm reminded how excited I was 16 years ago to see what he'd accomplish in his basketball career. I realize now that I might be even more excited to see what he'll do when basketball is over. Having already built a singular legacy, LeBron James has the rest of his life to add to it. The potential impact is massive. There's still nothing average about him.

—Ryan Jones, former editor-in-chief of *SLAM* magazine and author of *King James, Believe the Hype: The LeBron James Story*

★ ★ ★
Introduction

NBA Legacy Power Rankings are a new conversational metric designed to account for individual achievement, team success, and longevity as an All-Star caliber player. It is a tool that could be used in debate format to compare Hall of Fame players across generations. Based on a calculation of NBA MVPs, championships, and All-Star seasons, *LeBron James vs. The NBA* uses these Legacy Points to rank the best players in NBA history from 15–1. These Legacy Points also suggest a path forward for LeBron James to enter the conversation of greatest player of all-time by his eventual retirement.

After leading his Cleveland Cavaliers to the 2016 NBA championship, this book offers a snapshot of where James currently ranks in terms of all-time Legacy Points. It details what he needs to specifically still accomplish to lay claim to the all-time throne, along with providing the case for why he'll get it done. This is described while diving deep into moments, games, seasons, and highlights from each legend's Hall of Fame story as well as doing the same for LeBron. The legends featured in this book extend from Bob Cousy in the 1950s through Kobe Bryant, who retired in 2016, while offering a snapshot of every other decade of NBA basketball in between.

Before analytics, set shots were strongly encouraged. Behind-the-back passes were considered showboating and defensive players were taught to never leave their feet to block an opposing shot. The three-point line was added in 1979, goaltending rules have evolved and changed, hand-checking was eliminated, point guards started dunking, centers now shoot threes, and many other changes to an ever-growing sport must be considered when comparing the best to ever live. There was also a time before the 1950 NBA season when only white players were allowed to earn a living in the League. But basketball, our sport, like our culture, continues to push forward and drive change. We've attempted to highlight leaders like Bill Russell, Kareem Abdul-Jabbar, and many others, like James, who dedicated their lives to helping make those societal improvements throughout this book.

NBA Legacy Points and their associated Power Rankings attempt to neutralize the evolution of the game to some degree, and focus on a finite portfolio of specific accomplishments (i.e. MVPs, championships, All-Star games) for each player. As you read on, feel free to tweet at @BowersCLE to share your opinions, displeasure, or general thoughts on this new metric for comparing the very best to ever play the sport that we all love so very much.

Chapter 1

★ ★ ★

The Numbers

So, Legacy Points. How does it work? What is it we're actually looking at here, and how do we arrive at these points?

Legacy Points: The MVP Factor

A player must win at least one NBA MVP award to qualify for the NBA Legacy Power Rankings, or activate their NBA Legacy Points. The NBA awarded its first Most Valuable Player trophy to Bob Pettit of the St. Louis Hawks in 1956. He is one of 13 players who went on to win the MVP more than once during the 60-plus seasons that followed. This growing collection of superstars—voted the most valuable player in the League after each regular season—are the only players eligible for the NBA Legacy Power Rankings.

Despite the potentially subjective nature of MVP voting, it's still important for your legacy as an NBA player to actually win one—especially if your goal is to be considered among the GOATs. Top 30 all-time caliber players like John Havlicek, Jerry West, Elgin Baylor, Jason Kidd, and Dwyane Wade, for example, did not win an MVP trophy. Considering West finished as the runner-up in MVP voting four times, and did enough to inspire the NBA logo, his omission from this list, along with others like him, could certainly be questioned. But for as brilliant as these Hall of Famers were, West, Havlicek, Baylor, Kidd, and Wade are not considered the single greatest player in basketball history. The NBA Legacy Power Rankings attempt to isolate the handful of elite players who are truly in that conversation, specifically.

To be considered the GOAT you have to win at least one MVP. Kareem Abdul-Jabbar won six, Bill Russell and Michael Jordan won five. Magic Johnson, Larry Bird, and Moses Malone won three. Shaquille O'Neal, Tim Duncan, Kobe Bryant, and LeBron James each won one or more. You cannot be considered the single greatest player in NBA history without being named the single greatest player in the League for at least one season. The goal of the NBA Legacy Power Ranking is to identify the handful of elite players who are truly in the conversation for Greatest of All-Time.

The Book of Basketball

In Bill Simmons' classic, *The Book of Basketball*, he famously ranks the greatest players of all-time much more comprehensively, while also weaving in his masterful brand of storytelling. Simmons' book, published in 2009, is widely considered the authority on overall all-time NBA player rankings. After creating and finalizing the NBA Legacy Power Rankings, I flipped back through the hardback version of *TBOB* to compare the names on each list. My findings are summarized below to offer some context for the Legacy Points introduced in this book.

- While not in the same order, 12 of *TBOB*'s top 15 players are represented in the top 15 spots on the NBA Legacy Power Ranking.
- The three players Simmons had in his top 15 in 2009 who are not eligible for the NBA Legacy Power Rankings are West (No. 8), Havlicek (No. 13), and Baylor (No. 14).
- Of the top 15 players on the NBA Legacy Power Rankings list, only three fall outside the top 15 in *TBOB* in 2009 (Julius Erving No. 16, LeBron James No. 20, and Bob Cousy No. 21)

Precise Levels of Greatness

Every achievement is worth certain amounts of Legacy Points. For instance, a player earns seven Legacy Points for every regular season MVP award they win.

Legacy Points Breakdown:
- MVP award: 7 points
- NBA championship: 10 points
- NBA All-Star: 3 points

Kevin Garnett, as an example, won an NBA championship as a member of the Boston Celtics. He also won an MVP as a member of the Minnesota Timberwolves. During his professional career, Garnett was a 15-time All-Star. Those accomplishments combine to rank KG No. 15 on the NBA Legacy Power Rankings list with 62 Legacy Points.

Kevin Garnett—Legacy Points: 62

- MVP award: 1 (7 Points)
- NBA championship: 1 (10 Points)
- NBA All-Star: 15 (45 Points)

LeBron James' Legacy Points through the 2017 All-Star Game

LeBron James' Legacy Points summarize four MVP Awards (28 points), three NBA championships (30 points), and 13 All-Star games (39 points). This ranks James directly ahead of Shaquille O'Neal (92) at No. 9 all-time heading into the 2017 playoffs. James would need to earn 40 more Legacy Points to match Michael Jordan with 137. Jordan won five MVPs, six championships, and was named to 14 All-Star games.

Michael Jordan—Legacy Points: 137

- MVP awards: 5 (35 Points)
- NBA championships: 6 (60 Points)
- NBA All-Star: 14 (42 Points)

NBA Legacy Power Rankings (February 2017)

All-Time Legend	MVPs	LPs (x7)	MVP Legacy Points	All-Stars	LPs (x3)	All-Star LPs	Rings	LPs (x10)	Ring LPs	LEGACY POINTS TOTAL
Bill Russell	5	7	35	12	3	36	11	10	110	181
Kareem Abdul-Jabbar	6	7	42	19	3	57	6	10	60	159
Michael Jordan	5	7	35	14	3	42	6	10	60	137
Kobe Bryant	1	7	7	18	3	54	5	10	50	111
Tim Duncan	2	7	14	15	3	45	5	10	50	109
Magic Johnson	3	7	21	12	3	36	5	10	50	107

LEBRON JAMES VS. THE NBA

All-Time Legend	MVPs	LPs (x7)	MVP Legacy Points	All-Stars	LPs (x3)	All-Star LPs	Rings	LPs (x10)	Ring LPs	LEGACY POINTS TOTAL
Bob Cousy	1	7	7	13	3	39	6	10	60	106
Julius Erving*	4	7	28	16	3	48	3	10	30	106
LeBron James	4	7	28	13	3	39	3	10	30	97
Shaquille O'Neal	1	7	7	15	3	45	4	10	40	92
Wilt Chamberlain	4	7	28	13	3	39	2	10	20	87
Larry Bird	3	7	21	12	3	36	3	10	30	87
Moses Malone	3	7	21	13	3	39	1	10	10	70
Hakeem Olajuwon	1	7	7	12	3	36	2	10	20	63
Kevin Garnett	1	7	7	15	3	45	1	10	10	62
Bob Pettit	2	7	14	11	3	33	1	10	10	57
David Robinson	1	7	7	10	3	30	2	10	20	57
Karl Malone	2	7	14	14	3	42	0	10	0	56
Dirk Nowitzki	1	7	7	13	3	39	1	10	10	56
Oscar Robertson	1	7	7	12	3	36	1	10	10	53
Dave Cowens	1	7	7	8	3	24	2	10	20	51
Willis Reed	1	7	7	7	3	21	2	10	20	48
Stephen Curry	2	7	14	4	3	12	2	10	20	46
Bob McAdoo	1	7	7	5	3	15	2	10	20	42
Kevin Durant	1	7	7	8	3	24	1	10	10	41
Allen Iverson	1	7	7	11	3	33	0	10	0	40
Charles Barkley	1	7	7	11	3	33	0	10	0	40
Steve Nash	2	7	14	8	3	24	0	10	0	38
Bill Walton	1	7	7	2	3	6	2	10	20	33
Wes Unseld	1	7	7	5	3	15	1	10	10	32
Russel Westbrook	1	7	7	6	3	18	0	10	0	25
Derrick Rose	1	7	7	3	3	9	0	10	0	16

Julius Erving won one NBA MVP to qualify for this list, along with winning one NBA championship and 11 All-Star appearances (50 Legacy Points). He also won three ABA MVPs and two ABA championships before arriving in the League. He was awarded Legacy Points for his ABA MVPs (21) and championships (20), along with five ABA All-Star appearances (15) to total 106 Legacy Points. Players like Connie Hawkins, however, who won an ABA MVP but not an NBA MVP, did not qualify for this list.

NBA Legacy Power Rankings Top 15

No. 15 – Kevin Garnett (62 Legacy Points)

No. 14 – Hakeem Olajuwon (63 Legacy Points)

No. 13 – Moses Malone (70 Legacy Points)

No. 12 – Wilt Chamberlain (87 Legacy Points)

No. 11 – Larry Bird (87 Legacy Points)

No. 10 – Shaquille O'Neal (92 Legacy Points)

No. 9 – LeBron James (97 Legacy Points)

No. 8 – Bob Cousy (106 Legacy Points)

No. 7 – Julius Erving (106 Legacy Points)

No. 6 – Magic Johnson (107 Legacy Points)

No. 5 – Tim Duncan (109 Legacy Points)

No. 4 – Kobe Bryant (111 Legacy Points)

No. 3 – Michael Jordan (137 Legacy Points)

No. 2 – Kareem Abdul-Jabbar (159 Legacy Points)

No. 1 – Bill Russell (181 Legacy Points)

NBA Three-Point Era (1979–present)

Kareem Abdul-Jabbar won the last of his six most valuable player awards during the 1979–80 season. Michael Jordan began his NBA career in 1984. Since Jordan made his first NBA All-Star team in 1985, no player has earned more than the 137 Legacy Points that MJ totaled during the three-point era of NBA basketball. Kobe Bryant totaled 111 Legacy Points during the three-point era while Tim Duncan retired with 109 Legacy Points and Shaq 92. After being voted as an All-Star starter in 2017, LeBron had totaled 97 Legacy Points heading into the 2017 Playoffs.

Chapter 2

★ ★ ★

From Phenom to NBA Rookie of the Year

The high school basketball prospects who competed at the 2001 ABCD camp in Teaneck, New Jersey, were seated in a college classroom when Los Angeles Lakers All-Star and reigning NBA champion Kobe Bryant arrived. Before teaming with Shaquille O'Neal to win multiple titles, Bryant would make his name at prestigious national camps like the one he'd now address. He was only five years removed from being the No. 13 overall pick in the 1996 Draft. As the three-time All-Star spoke, a junior from Akron, Ohio, named LeBron James who was beginning to contemplate that same prep-to-pro leap, sat in the audience.

"If you look at the draft this year, you see a bunch of high school players coming out," Bryant began to explain, as captured by the documentary crews chronicling the Adidas ABCD Camp for an ESPN *The Life* episode that first aired on the network in 2001. "They want to blame me, they want to blame Kevin, they want to blame Tracy, but it's happening. But the main thing I want to tell you guys is, don't put all of your eggs in one basket. What I mean by that, is don't let people make the decision for you. Don't let people say, well he has to go pro because he's that great already. Do whatever you want to do. If you want to go to Stanford, go to Stanford. If you want to go to Duke, go to Duke. If you want to go to the pros, go to the pros. Don't let them tell you what you can or can not do. Don't rely on basketball for your happiness, because it's not going to happen. You have to make sure you balance your life out, you got something there for yourself in life, you get your education right. And on the basketball court just rip hearts out."

The ESPN segment features two New York City phenoms named Sebastian Telfair and Lenny Cooke. Telfair, a sophomore at Abraham Lincoln High School at the time, would later go on to be selected with the No. 13 pick in 2004 and played over a dozen years in the League. Cooke, considered by some as the best player in the 2002 class, would see his promising career tragically derail off the court. The third high school player who was profiled in the piece was 16-year-old LeBron.

"I don't want to be like Kobe Bryant," James said two years before declaring for the NBA draft. "I just want to accomplish the things that he accomplished. Like winning the championship, All-Stars, just doing those things."

An NBA Rookie of the Year from Akron

A 6'8" forward from Baltimore named Carmelo Anthony was among the many talented players who joined James and others at sneaker giant Sonny Vaccaro's ABCD camp in 2001. A 6'11" center from Texas named Chris Bosh was also in attendance. Those three players would be selected among the top four picks in what many consider one of the greatest drafts in NBA history two years later. That NBA class would also welcome Dwyane Wade with the fifth overall pick, and nine future All-Stars overall.

The expectations for James as he began his professional career were unlike any high school player making the leap to the League before him. Kevin Garnett was selected with the fifth overall pick, for example, and Bryant the 13th. But since the talent evaluators began to suggest that LeBron would be not just an NBA player, not just an All-Star, not just a champion, not just an MVP, but also potentially the greatest player to ever live, the hype only continued to grow to seemingly impossible expectations. But James would answer the critics immediately in his first NBA game.

The second half of an ESPN NBA double-header to begin the 2003–04 season matched the Cleveland Cavaliers first overall pick against the Kings in Sacramento. Peja Stojokovic scored the first three points of LeBron's first NBA game when he collected a Mike Bibby pass to bury a triple on the left wing. The first assist for James would come a couple trips later when he lofted an alley oop that Ricky Davis deposited through the rim for two. James' first field goal attempt

St. Vincent-St. Mary High School star LeBron James plays on January 13, 2002, at the Cleveland Convocation Center in Cleveland. (AP Photo/Tony Dejak)

in NBA history was pure from the right baseline about 15 feet from the basket. The bucket cut the Kings lead to 7–6. He'd make his second shot from about the same distance but from the left baseline, and then soar through the NBA sky for his first professional slam with 3:03 remaining in the opening period. He'd total 19 points and eight assists on 9-of–14 shooting through three quarters before finishing with 25 points, nine assists, and six rebounds in a 106–92 loss.

"I'll tell you what, he's much better than I thought he was going to be," Sean Elliot, who was calling the game, said of James as the contest concluded. "I'm going to tell all the NBA players right now, he's much better than you think he is."

James was still a couple months away from his 19th birthday when he played the first NBA game of his rookie season. His highly anticipated debut is largely considered not just the best debut of any teenager in League history, but also the best debut of anyone who ever played—especially considering the coverage and conversation surrounding the young prodigy as he entered the game. James' point total in his debut would far exceed the combined professional debuts of Kevin Garnett, Kobe Bryant, and Tracy McGrady, who scored eight between them.

A Season of Firsts and Milestones

LeBron scored 25 points in his NBA debut and then followed that up the next night in Phoenix with 21 points, 12 rebounds, and eight assists. He'd score 20 or more points 40 times as a first year pro for the Cleveland Cavaliers, and 30 or more points 20 times before his 20th birthday. On March 27, 2004, James recorded his season high when he gave the New Jersey Nets 41 in a three-point Cavaliers victory.

In a double-overtime loss to the Memphis Grizzlies on November 29, 2003, James reached the 30-point plateau for the first time as a pro. Playing against a starting five that included Pau Gasol, Mike Miller, and Jason Williams, James finished with 33 points, 16 rebounds, and seven assists. It was his 17th NBA game. He'd go for 37 at home against Paul Pierce and the Boston Celtics a couple weeks later, before getting 36 and 32 in back-to-back games at Philadelphia and Chicago. During that same month of December, James went for 34 against Tracy McGrady and the Orlando Magic and 32 against Portland. In February, after celebrating his 19th birthday weeks earlier, LeBron would go on to get 38 at Washington, 32 at home against the Lakers, and then 32, 30, 34, and 34 against the Spurs, Magic, Hawks, and Warriors before securing NBA Rookie of the Year honors without debate.

LeBron at his introductory news conference on Friday, June 27, 2003, at Gund Arena in Cleveland. (AP Photo/Tony Dejak)

"To the other rookies," LeBron said toward the end of his ROY acceptance speech, "I felt like it was going to be a close race between me and Carmelo. I was able to win the award, but he had a phenomenal season also. Dwayne Wade had a phenomenal season, and for those two teams [Denver and Miami] to be in the playoffs means a lot to me. Other rookies—Chris Bosh and Kirk Hinrich—made an impact in this league. This might be the best rookie class since 1995."

Young LeBron Scores 41

LeBron James matched up with future Cavaliers teammate Richard Jefferson and the New Jersey Nets on March 27, 2004. The Nets were 42–29 on the year, the Cavs 31–40. Earlier in the season, James scored as many as 30 points in an NBA game for the first time in a double-overtime thriller against the Grizzlies. He'd score 30-plus points in regulation for the first time ever against the Boston Celtics on December 13, 2003. But after taking the court alongside friend and teammate Zydrunas Ilgauskas at Gund Arena against the Nets, James would score 40 for the first time.

James scored only two points in the first quarter on the night he got 40 for the first time in the League. He'd total 25 through three quarters before scoring 15 points in the fourth to reach a game- and career-high of 41. His Cavaliers would need every one of those points, too, as a James finish at the rim with 1.9 seconds remaining made it 107–104 Cleveland. Veteran guard Kerry Kittles attempted a 42-foot heave as the final buzzer sounded that fell short, and Cleveland escaped with a hard-fought victory, earned on the strength of their young superstar.

The true brilliance of LeBron's all-around skill-set was on display for one of the first times that night in Cleveland when LeBron scored 41 as a rookie. Even while hanging such a big number in the scoring column, James also dominated all other phases of the game at the same time. He'd dish out 13 dimes against the Nets and grab six rebounds while also pilfering three steals. As would prove to be the case throughout his career, James would efficiently arrive at his game-high scoring total by shooting 15-of-29 from the floor. He'd log 43 minutes, make one of two three-pointers, and knock down all 10 of the free throws he attempted. Big Z finished with 17 and 10 while Jefferson paced his Nets long before his Snapchat career with 35, seven, and six in a losing effort.

By the end of his first professional season, James would join Carmelo Anthony, Chris Bosh, and Dwyane Wade on the All-Rookie First team. Like Michael Jordan, Shaquille O'Neal, Tim Duncan, and the many legends before him, LeBron's exploits would earn him NBA Rookie of the Year Honors. He averaged 20.9 points, 5.9 assists, and 5.5 rebounds. Meanwhile, Carmelo averaged 21 points and 6.1 rebounds as a rookie for Denver, Bosh 11.5 and 7.4 for Toronto, and Wade 16.2 points and 4.5 assists for Miami. In his opening act as an NBA superstar, LeBron offered a resounding statement of authentic greatness that would put him on a crash course with his first NBA All-Star game.

Chapter 3

★ ★ ★

LeBron James vs. Kevin Garnett

Professional Career: 1995–2007
NBA: Minnesota Timberwolves, Boston Celtics, Brooklyn Nets, Minnesota Timberwolves
Legacy Points: 62 (No. 15)

Kevin Garnett was a transcendent figure in NBA history. While following a trail first blazed by Moses Malone, Garnett reignited a youth movement in the NBA that resulted in an explosion of 20-year-old millionaires calling "Next!" across the Association. Like traditional 7-foot superstars who dominated the NBA before him, KG proved throughout his career to be a difference-maker defending the rim and anchoring the paint. Like the traditional bigs offensively, he could get his with his back to the basket, too, while stepping out to hit from 15. But unlike those before him, KG had guard skills. He brought the ball up the floor, dunked on your head, and then rejected your layup jogging back down on the other end. He was the Big Ticket.

Garnett dominated the game differently than NBA centers dominated it before him. Even before the social media age, Garnett was known across America the moment he declared for the 1995 NBA Draft as a high school senior in Chicago. I was entering the ninth grade when KG arrived in Cleveland that summer for an AAU tournament at a local high school. His Team Detroit won big against a collection of legitimate stars on an AAU squad named Team Pittsburgh. Several D-I college players occupied this summer league roster opposite Garnett, led by Cleveland legend and Cincinnati Bearcats Hall of Famer Melvin "The Helicopter" Levett.

That was the first time I saw Kevin Garnett play basketball. Our ninth grade AAU team had just finished a game in a nearby gym. We sat in our uniforms as little kids watching a player we saw on ESPN who was about to enter the NBA out of high school. Our coach wanted to make sure we saw him. We heard this player ask a gym packed with major college coaches and several dozen NBA scouts what style of dunk they wanted to see next as he dribbled the ball at half court. Three sixty was the answer, and he promptly delivered at the hoop we were sitting under. It was the single greatest thing I had ever seen in my life. It was also the first time LeBron James saw Kevin Garnett play, too, as he'd mention years later in an Instagram tribute to KG upon his retirement.

"I mean, where do I start?" LeBron said. "First watching you play at the Solon Cage Classic in Ohio with Team Michigan when u were in HS, I believe I was 10 years old and I was like dang this dude nice!! Then a lil time passed and u were drafted straight out of HS to the pros so I felt like man whoever get him is a lucky team. And I surely wasn't wrong! The KID nickname was fly, swaged out and made a 10 year old kid from Akron believe he could run with the big boys himself! Fast forward 8 years later that kid you inspired entered the draft fresh out of HS as well. Thank you!"

LeBron vs. Kevin Garnett

Legacy Power Rankings: 97 vs. 62

Garnett:

- **MVP award: 1 (7)**
- **NBA championship: 1 (10)**
- **NBA All-Star: 15 (45)**

For as great as Garnett was, LeBron won more championships. He also won three more MVPs, while executing a blueprint the Big Ticket had just delivered on how to make it in the NBA directly out of high school. Had KG been less reluctant to give in to the idea of a trade to Boston during his last few seasons in Minnesota, and formed a Big Three sooner, he would've won more rings. But Garnett didn't win big until he got to Boston, and their epic run resulted in one banner raised forever in Boston.

Chapter 4

★ ★ ★

First All-Star Game

LeBron James earned 1,661,204 fan votes to appear in his first NBA All-Star Game during his second professional season. Shaquille O'Neal led all Eastern Conference players with 2,488,089 million votes after being traded from the Los Angeles Lakers to the Miami Heat. Houston Rockets center Yao Ming—with the help of avid NBA fans in his native China—led the Western Conference stars in 2005 with the most ASG votes overall (2,558,578). Minnesota Timberwolves forward Kevin Garnett was the only other player to exceed 2 million votes. Alongside James and O'Neal for the East starters, opposite Yao, KG, Tim Duncan, Kobe Bryant, and Tracy McGrady, were fellow future Hall of Famers Allen Iverson, Grant Hill, and Vince Carter.

Since Michael Jordan, Larry Bird, Charles Barkley, and the 1992 Olympic Dream Team helped make basketball a global sport, NBA rosters were being filled with an increasing number of international players. By 2005, six players selected to the 24 All-Star spots were born in a foreign country. Those included LeBron James' teammate Zydrunas Ilgauskas (Lithuania), Manu Ginobili (Argentina), Steve Nash (Canada), Dirk Nowitzki (Germany), Tim Duncan (U.S. Virgin Islands), and Yao Ming (China). Despite more and more players from around the world competing in the NBA than ever before, a 20-year-old LeBron still accounted for the eighth most All-Star votes of anyone on the planet. The high school prodigy from Akron was officially on his way to taking over the basketball world.

LeBron would walk through the lights and cameras out onto the NBA All-Star stage during the pregame introductions after Philadelphia 76ers legend Allen Iverson. James held his arms above his head making a rock symbol as an homage, or paid sponsorship, for Jay-Z's Rockafella Records Label. After throwing up the rock, LeBron took the court for the main event of the NBA's All-Star Weekend for the very first time. He'd start quickly, too, knocking down a 22-foot jumper near the top of the key to give his Eastern Conference squad an early 5–0 lead. Iverson then found James shortly after with a lob pass that the young Cavaliers superstar fiercely deposited. LeBron returned the favor, serving up a no-look dime to a cutting AI along the baseline from there, and then jumped the passing lane in the second half for a steal and high-flying fast break finish. The rim-rattling jam led TNT analyst and future coach of the Golden State Warriors, Steve Kerr, to exclaim in response, "Speaking of athletic, watch this!"

With the NBA community watching from inside the Pepsi Center in Denver and around the globe to see how the reigning Rookie of the Year would perform on the All-Star stage, LeBron finished with 13 points, eight rebounds, six assists, and two steals. As he'd continue to do on basketball's biggest stages for the next decade and beyond, James contributed in all phases of the game just as he did during the season for his Cavaliers. He was a proven scorer and exceptional athlete who could get 40 on any given night—even as a second-year pro. But at the same time, he was also making all the right basketball plays.

He was different, in the sense that he wasn't the volume scorer that NBA fans had become accustomed to seeing. He was in position to collect rebounds, he could see the floor better than anyone else, his basketball IQ was elite, and he could score in a variety of ways even while still working on developing a more consistent outside shot. The following season, James would return to win his first All-Star Game MVP. Two years later, in 2008, he'd win a second ASG MVP. But in LeBron's first appearance, it was Iverson who hoisted that trophy above his head. The Hall of Famer finished with 15 points and 10 assists as LeBron's East beat the West 125–115.

Following the game, when asked why he deferred to other teammates throughout the contest instead of attempting to takeover, James told the media, "My time in these games will come."

One year later, he'd become the youngest All-Star Game MVP in NBA history.

All-Star Impact in Cleveland

LeBron James improved his scoring average by 6.3 points during his second season in the Association. He'd also improve his assists by 1.3 per contest and rebounds by 1.9. He finished his sophomore campaign at 27.2 points, 7.4 rebounds, and 7.2 assists. His first All-Star season would also be his first exceeding the 27/7/7 mark that he averaged for his career through his first 1,000 games in the NBA. The majority of James' improvement in the scoring column, specifically, was built on improving his efficiency—something that he'd relentlessly pursue throughout the remainder of his career. LeBron took better shots, from better spots on the floor, at 20 than he did at 19. He was also beginning to understand how opposing defenses were game planning to attack him on a nightly basis. He was a smart player with unique talent who was also willing to put in the work to be great. He quickly began to elevate his Cleveland franchise as a direct result of his individual improvement.

James finished his second season in the League by increasing his overall field goal percentage by a staggering six points (41.7 percent as a rookie to 47.2 percent), while also shooting a respectable 35.1 percent from three. His rookie season ended with a career-low 29 percent three-point percentage while adjusting from the high school to professional three-point line, but he was showing improvement. While more of an average three-point shooter in his second season, LeBron had improved enough from deep to keep defenders at least honest. They had to come out and contest LeBron's triple, which helped open up avenues to the basket for the young King to exploit as a result.

LeBron shot 75 percent from the free throw line, too, while also improving his turnovers in Year Two for the Cavs. This individual performance, combined with an improving Cavs record, was enough to suggest that LeBron already belonged among the game's elite before he was of legal age to purchase alcohol. But regardless of where you sided in that debate, there was no denying his impact at the box office. After averaging less than 12,000 fans per night during the season before LeBron arrived in the NBA, the Cavaliers were averaging over 19,000 fans during the first All-Star season of James' career. The additional 7,000 fans he single-handedly drew were lining the franchise and League with increased revenue every time he stepped onto the floor. The fans were packing not only Gund Arena in

Downtown Cleveland, but also every opposing arena the Cavs played—and he was just getting started.

New Heights for a Young King

LeBron James scored 40 or more points five different times during the 2004–05 season. His highest scoring game as a rookie was 41, but he only hit the 40-or-more mark once. But he'd demonstrate his ability as an elite scorer well enough to hit 40 with more regularity in his second season, and his legend only grew because of it.

Those five times he exceeded this threshold during his second season with the Cavaliers are listed below as a reference:

- **40 Points** vs. Atlanta Hawks on December 28, 2004, in a nine-point Cleveland win.
- **40 Points** vs. Milwaukee Bucks on April 9, 2005, in a 17-point Cleveland win.
- **43 Points** vs. Detroit Pistons on November 24, 2004, in a 16-point Cleveland win.
- **44 Points** vs. New Orleans on March 28, 2005, in a one-point Cleveland win.
- **56 Points** vs. Toronto Raptors on March 20, 2005, in a seven-point Toronto win.

Young LeBron Scores Half a Hundred in Toronto

As the 2003 No. 1 overall pick, the NBA's rookie scale contract paid LeBron James $4.3 million during his second season. Zydrunas Ilgauskas, one of Cleveland's two All-Stars that year, averaged 16.9 points and 8.6 rebounds. He was the highest paid player on the Cavaliers roster, earning $14.6 million in 2004–05. Despite firing respected veteran Coach Paul Silas after Dan Gilbert purchased the team with 18 games to go, the Cavs finished with a record of 42–40. It would represent a seven-game improvement over the previous season, despite falling short of the postseason.

On March 20, the Cavaliers were 34–29 when they arrived at the Air Canada Centre to take on the 27–38 Toronto Raptors. Current ESPN NBA analyst Jalen Rose was arguably the team's best player that season, with an improving Chris

Vince Carter and LeBron James during East team practice for the 2005 NBA All-Star Game. (AP Photo/Mark J. Terrill)

Bosh not far behind. Rose would finish that game with 30 points while Bosh added 11. But the night, even in a losing effort, belonged to James, who poured in 56. He attempted 36 field goals in the contest and made 18. He'd also shoot 50 percent from three-point range, connecting on 6-of-12 threes along with 14 of 15 free throws. He'd collect more rebounds than Rose, Bosh, or any other Raptor besides Donyell Marshall, too, finishing the night with 10 boards to go along with five assists. But even with Cavs teammate Drew Gooden going for 24 and 10 in support of the King, the Cavaliers fell short on the road.

Cleveland trailed by only one point heading into the final period, but was out-lasted by Toronto, who extended their lead by six during the fourth before securing the 105–98 victory. But that didn't diminish James' brilliance earlier, like when he buried a deep three to cut the deficit in half as the first quarter sounded, or gutted the Raptors defense with a high-flying smash in the half court. Or, like when he beat Rose to score points 49 and 50 for the very first time in his NBA career. Despite the loss, and the losing early on, LeBron James continued to score from there and he hasn't stopped since.

Chapter 5

★ ★ ★

Evolution of LeBron: Ricky Davis Effect

LeBron James learned many lessons from his teammates throughout his NBA career. This process began during his first season as a member of the Cleveland Cavaliers. He'd join forces with a young Carlos Boozer as well as longtime teammate Zydrunas Ilguaskas. He'd learn lessons about how to build a roster as well as how to conduct yourself in the NBA. James would also learn lessons that would help form his role as a team leader over much of the next decade from his interactions with NBA veteran scorer Ricky Davis.

LeBron crosses paths with Davis at an interesting point in NBA history. Magic Johnson's ball-sharing brand of dominant basketball, which could also be found in many elements of Larry Bird's game, was quickly overshadowed by Michael Jordan's dominance in the years that followed Magic and Bird's reign over the NBA. (Bird and Johnson won six MVPs in seven seasons.) Why this is important is because Jordan was the NBA's most ruthless scorer. Jordan's scoring was so dominant it overshadowed the well-rounded nature of his game. MJ was a fierce perimeter defender. He could distribute the basketball and was willing to trust his teammates with the game on the line (i.e., Steve Kerr, John Paxson, Craig Hodges, etc.). But what a high school age Kobe Bryant and Kevin Garnett saw on ESPN was the scoring. To be great at NBA basketball you had to score the ball. That was the message. Ricky Davis was a young baller who hoped to use the game to better his life and he heard this message too.

Davis spent his basketball career trying to get as many buckets as he could. Kobe Bryant had the same approach, he was just a markedly better basketball player in all areas of the game than Ricky D. But we are making a mistake as sports fans or pundits when we discount the fact that players like Davis are just trying to be as aggressive as they possibly can by scoring the ball. He was getting paid millions of dollars, in part, because he was able to score consistently in the NBA even if he was on a bad team. Or especially if he was on a bad team.

The Cavs were a bad team when LeBron James arrived and Ricky Davis was the squad's leading scorer. He thought the same way all the great scorers thought when a young playmaker arrived. Davis thought the Cavaliers had drafted James to help him score the ball with more efficiency and regularity. Bryant would have had the same thought if the Lakers drafted James. It would have made sense for Kobe to think that because he was much better than Davis. But Ricky D was earning crazy bank for what he'd been able to accomplish in his professional career since his time in the Big Ten with Iowa, and why exactly should he change the mental approach that got him there and jeopardize all that?

So that's why Ricky Davis wasn't wrong for being selfish from an individual standpoint. But the Cavaliers obviously did not draft LeBron to help Ricky D get buckets. The result of this miscommunication was a lack of on-court chemistry between the Cavs leading scorer and the franchise player they just drafted. In different ways, this dynamic between Davis and James and the organization would cause significant challenges for the team during their first year together.

There is a famous story that is told among Cavaliers staffers that describes the time that Davis left practice and in his Cavs practice gear stood in line at a concession stand inside of what was then Gund Arena to purchase and eat a hot dog while mingling with fans who were also in line while attending the Circus. That type of behavior is not necessarily conducive to developing rookies. James took this experience and has consistently tried to reach out to rookies and make them feel welcome throughout his time as a reigning MVP and champion ever since. James understood from his relationship with Davis how it can feel—even as a rookie starter—to be frozen out at times from the veterans for reasons that don't even really concern you as a person specifically. But James also saw firsthand how an NBA veteran should always try to give back even if nobody else is looking.

There is also a famous story in Cavs circles about the time the team was filming a promotional spot with LeBron and Ricky Davis during their first year together. James was on his rookie contract at the time but Davis was making above the League minimum. As the story goes, there was a homeless person who was watching the entire shoot. After it was over, Davis took off his sneakers and autographed them for the man. He then reached into his bag and pulled out a wad of cash that was in a rubber band. He popped the money inside the shoe and gave it to the guy. The response from the homeless man that Ricky Davis handed roughly $5K inside his Nike shoe after filming a team spot was reportedly indescribable. Selfish, silly, class clowning, or otherwise, Ricky D was a good guy just doing a job who helped out those less fortunate whenever he could. LeBron saw all that from Ricky D too.

LeBron, Ricky D, and the Cavs

Ricky Davis spent 22 games as LeBron's teammate during James' rookie season before he was traded away for all of the reasons cited above to the Boston Celtics. In LeBron's first ever game against the Sacramento Kings on October 29, 2003, Davis totaled 14 points and five assists. During James first ever NBA win, on November 8 against the Washington Wizards, Ricky posted 26 points, eight rebounds, and five assists on 9-of-15 shooting from the field. He'd also score 25 in back-to-back games against the Detroit Pistons and Memphis Grizzlies, and went for a Cavs season-high of 27 against the Los Angeles Clippers.

Davis started 22 games alongside LeBron before being traded to the Boston Celtics in December 2003. He'd only start in five of the 56 games he'd play for the Celtics, coming off the bench as a second unit scorer for Boston. Davis would spend six more seasons in the NBA. He'd appear in games for the Minnesota Timberwolves and Los Angeles Clippers before retiring at 30 years old in 2010. Davis played in over 700 regular season NBA games and averaged 13.5 points per game since arriving in 1998 as a 19-year-old who believed he could score on anybody and was determined to prove specifically that.

Lessons in Leadership

LeBron James may not have at first looked more like Magic Johnson than Michael Jordan if he did not have a personality like Ricky Davis on his team. There were many things that LeBron was forced to adjust to upon arrival in the NBA. He had to handle the finances for himself and his family, he had to produce on the floor, he had to learn the NBA game, learn his opponents, learn from his coaches, and win. Navigating through Ricky Davis for more shot attempts was properly shelved by a young James until after the organization had a chance to trade him.

There is also an obvious theme in regards to how James has treated rookies and new teammates. They quickly have a handshake that is demonstrated for all on the sideline, they feel welcome, they grow as players. The Davis experience helped even a player as talented and ready to produce in the NBA as James learn that championship teammates do not create those type of rifts.

Chapter 6

★ ★ ★

LeBron James vs. Hakeem Olajuwon

Professional Career: 1984–2002
NBA: Houston Rockets, Toronto Raptors
Legacy Points: 63 (No. 14)

Googling LeBron and Hakeem Olajuwon serves up a YouTube video from 2013 of a basketball training session in which Hakeem teaches LeBron post moves in a gym during the NBA off-season. Specifically, he helps James incorporate some elements of his signature move, the Dream Shake, into his game. Hakeem has done this regularly for many other NBA stars since he retired, helping the next generation of legends continue to develop and push the game further. "Well, I knew he worked guys out that wanted to get better and I wanted to expand my game," James told ESPN of his workouts with Olajuwon. "So, it's not hard for me to reach somebody, and I wanted to expand my game in the low post. I felt like if I could do that then I could be more dynamic and make our team better, so, couple phone calls here and I was able to make it happen."

Olajuwon entered the NBA as the No. 1 overall pick in the 1984 Draft. He was a shot-blocking savant, who dominated NCAA basketball as the anchor of a dunking machine known as the Houston Cougars. Throughout his professional career, Olajuwon continued to improve before ultimately blending unstoppable power around the rim

25

with the graceful footwork of a Premier League Futbol player. Hakeem was devastatingly precise, but fluid enough to adjust whenever needed. He would lead his Rockets to two NBA championships from 1994–95 while also winning one of two Defensive Player of the Year awards during Houston's stretch of superiority over the NBA.

During the 1995 NBA Playoffs, Olajuwon's Rockets defeated, in order: John Stockton and Karl Malone's Utah Jazz, Charles Barkley and Dan Majerle's Phoenix Suns, David Robinson and Avery Johnson's San Antonio Spurs, and then ultimately Shaquille O'Neal and Anfernee Hardaway's Orlando Magic in the Finals. Olajuwon averaged 33 points and 10.3 rebounds during those 22 postseason games on his way to a second-straight NBA championship. While receiving the basketball from point guard Kenny Smith, Olajuwon scored 45 points against the Jazz to open the postseason. He went for 36 and 11 during a 33-point victory over the Suns, 41 and 16 in a 10-point win over the Spurs, along with 35 and 15 to close out Shaq and the Magic in Game 4 for the sweep.

Hakeem's accomplishments on the basketball court and in life serve as an inspiration to many young people all over the world. Born in Nigeria, Olajuwon spoke English as a second language when he immigrated to the United States to enroll in college at Houston. In his own way, he'd rewrite the history of basketball with his dominance around the basket at both ends of the floor. He captured the painted area with his physical skill and strength, and then fortified its defense with strategy and balance. He was Hakeem "the Dream" for all the right reasons, an example of excellence and teamwork for us all.

LeBron vs. Hakeem Olajuwon

Legacy Power Rankings: 97 vs. 63
Olajuwon:
- **MVP award: 1 (7)**
- **NBA championship: 2 (20)**
- **NBA All-Star: 12 (36)**

Olajuwon continued to move the center position forward with his innovative play and strategic arsenal of moves around the basket. But LeBron James dominates a perimeter game that appears to be the forward trajectory of basketball. Or, more directly, despite winning back-to-back championships and dominating the NBA for two straight seasons, James passed Hakeem in the rings column with three by 2016. He also won two more MVPs by that point, while tying Olajuwon in All-Star games.

Chapter 7

★ ★ ★

LeBron James vs. Moses Malone

Professional Career: 1974–1995
ABA: Utah Stars, Spirits of St. Louis
NBA: Buffalo Braves, Houston Rockets, Philadelphia 76ers, Washington Bullets, Atlanta Hawks, Milwaukee Bucks, San Antonio Spurs
Legacy Points: 70 (No. 13)

Moses Malone led Petersburg High School in Virginia to 50 straight victories and back-to-back state titles before bypassing college basketball in search of a professional contract in 1974. During that reign of schoolboy dominance, the neighborhood ballers who populated the Petersburg playgrounds would only allow young Moses to play if he agreed to stay outside of the key during pickup games. The lanky 6'10" center who attacked the glass with what would later be called a relentless motor went on to become an NBA Hall of Famer from there. But the journey for Malone, as it is for all of basketball's great pioneers, was not easy.

Eventually, however—after battling large-scale public criticism which might have looked similar to the takes used as pitchforks by our modern-day Twitter mob presented as sports columns in newspapers across America—the only son of a hard-working woman who was forced to drop out of school in fifth grade to earn money for her family hit the basketball lottery. Following the 1982 NBA season, the Philadelphia 76ers—who had just lost in the Finals to Kareem Abdul-Jabbar and the Los Angeles Lakers—inked Malone to an offer sheet. The deal was worth an NBA record $13.2 million over six years. Malone won his second MVP award that season with the Houston Rockets, who had a right to match their restricted free agent's offer.

During his six years with the Rockets, following the ABA-NBA merger in 1976, Malone averaged 24 points and 15 rebounds. He would go on to become an NBA All-Star from 1978 to 1989, and lead the League in rebounding in '79 with 17.6 per game. Houston had every right to match the Sixers offer and hold on to their 26-year-old center who kept getting better every season. Instead, they'd let him walk, and orchestrate a sign-and-trade that would pair Malone with the great Julius "Dr. J" Erving and alter the fate of NBA history.

Erving had won the NBA MVP award in 1981, and Malone won it the following year with Houston. Now, the League's back-to-back MVPs would be on the same team and Philly would finally get over that hump. During Malone's first season with the Sixers, he averaged 24.5 and 15.3 while leading the League in rebounding once again. He'd also win his second straight MVP and third overall that year, while ending the season with a 4–0 sweep over the Lakers in the NBA Finals. After losing to Los Angeles in 1980 and 1982, the Sixers finally had the best player in the world that season at the center position and would be crowned NBA champions.

Malone spent four seasons in Philadelphia from 1982 to '86 before returning in 1993 to appear in 55 games. He'd appear in a total of 357 regular season games for the City of Brotherly Love in all, and average 21 points and 12 rebounds. They nicknamed him Chairman of the Boards because that's what he was. Rebounds appeared to be Moses Malone's birthright. He got them all. But Malone was much more than numbers, stats, titles, and trivia. He was an elite athlete, but he also represented a challenge. He dared to think outside the restraints of popular opinion. He forced many others to do the same with his success as a player who bypassed college amidst criticisms and went on to become not just a success story, but one of the very best players in NBA history.

Changing the Game

On Sunday, March 30, 1975, the *Lakeland Ledger* published an article about Malone during his first professional season with the Utah Stars. He bucked popular opinion by deciding to skip college basketball to instead earn a living to support his mother and family by entering pro basketball directly from high school. Nobody in his position had ever made that decision. In the past, everyone followed the rules. But these rules weren't keeping the lights on for Moses and his mother. So he signed a contract to play professional basketball in the ABA as a teenager and the professional journey began.

Moses Malone: From Scared Prep Player to Confident Pro (March 30, 1975, *Lakeland Ledger*):

A few months ago, ghetto-born Moses Malone was scratching pennies from his mother's meager household budget so he could buy milk for school lunch. Today, with more money than he ever imagined existed, he is awaiting delivery of a $10,000-plus Lincoln Continental with a built-in color television set. He is also getting reports on the construction project of a new $30,000 home he is building in St. Petersberg, VA, for his mother.

Sudden wealth came to Malone, a 19-year-old, 6-foot, 11-inch, 215 pounder, when, ignoring the blandishments of hundreds of college recruiters, he signed to play professional basketball with the Utah Stars. For becoming the first player ever in the 30-year history of professional basketball to jump directly from high school to the pros, Malone was given a million-dollar contract, $200,000 for five years.

Malone was the target of several steaming hot takes built around the façade of a college education, which was used in some cases to mask the ultimate jealousy of this young person's riches. While driving to work in that luxury Continental, Moses would average 18.8 points and 14.6 rebounds for Utah. He'd play parts of one more ABA season the following year with the Spirits of St. Louis before the league that drafted the first high school player in 30 years disbanded.

The following season, in 1976, Moses began an NBA career that lasted nearly two decades. He finished in the top 10 in rebounds during 14 different seasons and currently ranks third all-time with 17,834 boards. He finished in the top 10 in scoring seven times as well, and ranks No. 9 on the NBA career scoring list with 27,409 points. Despite being considered a "ghetto-born" kid who wasn't smart enough to realize he needed the invaluable experience of a college education in order to have a successful life, Moses Malone did it his way and did it just fine.

Farewell to a Giant

The great Moses Malone passed away from natural causes much too soon on September 13, 2015, having lived an actively engaged life of 60 years. He is remembered by his family, teammates, as well as every NBA fan that will ever live for his contribution to a League that so many fans treasure. He asked a question that changed the basketball world: How can you be too young to put food on your family's table if you are already capable of competing with the best in the world? For over two decades, Malone backed that dream up and made it possible for Kevin Garnett, Kobe Bryant, and LeBron James to eventually do the same.

"He was the first person that I actually got an opportunity to see my rookie year," LeBron James told the media of meeting he had early in his career with the prep-to-pro pioneer. "I ate pregame lunch with him, rookie year, before my first game in Sacramento. He came to my hotel room in Sacramento, we ate a pregame meal, just talked about what it's like to be a rookie in the league. He gave me a bunch of stories, and so it was very sad when I [saw] him pass. And, obviously, you know every time I saw him I called him Uncle Mo every time, because he was always just there for me."

LeBron vs. Moses Malone

Legacy Power Rankings: 97 vs. 70
Malone:
- **MVP award: 3 (21)**
- **NBA championship: 1 (10)**
- **NBA All-Star: 13 (39)**

The LeBron James that we know today might not exist without the success that Moses Malone was able to have at a young age as a professional basketball player both on and off the court. Malone opened the door for not only James, but all the prep-to-pro players who found great success in the NBA. Like James, Malone was also a superstar who made others around him better. He joined a team with an MVP in Dr. J. and a roster that had been to the NBA Finals twice before he arrived, and elevated the collective performance.

LEBRON JAMES VS. MOSES MALONE

LeBron earned more Legacy Points than Moses to rank higher on this Power Ranking list due to his championships and MVPs totals. If Houston had somehow broken through to win an additional title or two, or Malone ended up in Philly three seasons earlier, maybe he has three or four more rings to go along with everything else that he put on the board. Or, maybe everything played out exactly as it was supposed to, with Malone answering the call to be the special player and person a changing times required.

Chapter 8

★ ★ ★

First NBA Finals

The debate that will wage throughout basketball eternity surrounding the selection of LeBron James' single greatest game will always depend on perspective. His near-perfect night in Boston en route to his first NBA championship with the Miami Heat in 2012 remains planted in the conversation. His 32-point triple-double against the Spurs in Game 6 before winning again the next season is there as well. In Cleveland, three years later, he transformed from a supremely gifted NBA fighter to the ultimate of basketball warriors in Games 6 and 7 of the 2016 Finals. But even after watching him deliver Northeast Ohio its first championship in 52 years, it's difficult to top what the NBA world witnessed on May 31, 2007.

Game 5 of the 2007 Eastern Conference Finals was held at The Palace of Auburn Hills. In the same building that Chauncey Billups, Richard Hamilton, and Rasheed Wallace helped raise the 2004 NBA championship banner, James and his Cleveland Cavaliers would match up with the best team in the Eastern Conference. Led by Billups, Hamilton, and Wallace, the Detroit Pistons won 53 games during the regular season to earn the No. 1 seed in the East. The Cavaliers finished three back of the Pistons in the Central Division, the only other team in the conference to win at least 50 that season. After sweeping the Washington Wizards and eliminating the New Jersey Nets, James and the Cavs found themselves even with Detroit through four games. The winner of Game 5 would most likely advance to the NBA Finals.

The Pistons were firing on all cylinders as Game 5 began. Sparked by Billups, Detroit whipped the ball around, over, and through the Cavaliers early, while building a 26–19 lead on the strength of eight assists to only one turnover through the first 10 minutes of action. Cavs guard Damon Jones would collect a LeBron James pass to knock down a triple, however, as Cleveland entered the second down six. Trailing by that same margin with five minutes remaining in the half— James probed the defense before finding Zydrunas Ilgauskas under the basket, who converted the three-point play. Big Z would finish the night with 16 points and seven rebounds as the Cavaliers second-leading scorer behind James, who led Cleveland in points, rebounds, assists, and steals.

LeBron scored six points in the first quarter and seven more in the second to enter the locker room with 13 points at halftime. The powerful Detroit bunch, famous for being the only team in modern NBA history to win a championship without a dominant superstar, featured a balanced attack led by Billups, Hamilton, Wallace, and Tayshaun Prince. (That year they also had Chris Webber, who obviously wasn't the All-NBA First Team player he was in Sacramento by this time, but still totaled 20 points, eight rebounds, and a team-best plus/minus of +15 in Game 5 of the 2007 ECF.) They led the Cavs 52–51 heading into the second half. But a 22-year-old LeBron James, who would've been a senior at Ohio State University had he played his first four years out of high school in Columbus, would come out in an attack mode that would've beaten anybody.

LeBron scored the Cavaliers' final 25 points in the game to give his team a 109–107 Game 5 victory, on the road, against a former NBA championship team who played well in their quest to get back to the Finals. James scored the next four points from there, before Drew Gooden split a pair of free throws for the Cavs with 2:49 remaining in the fourth quarter to cut the Detroit lead to 88–84. Gooden would then collect a Hamilton miss at the other end, which led to a 26-foot three-pointer from the young King that found nothing but the bottom. The three James hit would inch the Cavaliers even closer, trailing now 88–87, before he then scored 25-straight points to win the game in double-overtime.

Two of James final 25 tied the game at 91–91 with two seconds remaining after Billups recaptured the lead momentarily with a triple of his own. LeBron would then do absolutely anything he wanted, while making the biggest basket of his professional career (to that point) roughly eight consecutive times on his way

Tim Duncan guards LeBron in the third quarter of Game 2 of the 2007 NBA Finals.
(AP Photo/Matt Slocum)

to the signature victory. He scored 18 points in the extra session to finish with 48 points, nine rebounds, seven assists, and two steals on 18-of-33 shooting from the field. This would also include the game's final basket, to put Cleveland ahead for good, 109–107. "We threw everything we had at him," Pistons guard Chauncey

Billups said of James following Game 5 of the ECF. "We just couldn't stop him. It's frustrating. He put on an unbelievable display out there. It's probably the best I have seen against us ever in the playoffs."

The Game 5 road victory gave LeBron and his Cavaliers a 3–2 advantage in the series. They closed the Pistons out at home two nights later by 16, and LeBron James had won his first Eastern Conference title long before even the lofty projections that followed him into the League had suggested.

James averaged 25.7 points, 9.2 rebounds, and 8.5 assists for the series while logging 277 minutes in six Eastern Conference Finals games. The next closest Cavalier in terms of playing time was Sasha Pavlovic at 203 minutes, followed by Ilgauskas at 194. After the game, Gooden referred to LeBron's performance as a "Video Game James" night. It was the best way to describe what we were all seeing for the first time.

"I was able to will my team to victory," James said after the game. "This is definitely a big win, one of the biggest wins in Cavaliers' franchise history. For me and my teammates, it's definitely the biggest win. But we have a goal, we can't dwell on this when we have another game on Saturday. We have got to do our best to try to win that ballgame and get where we wanted to be all year."

2006–07 Cleveland Cavaliers

LeBron's 2007 Cleveland Cavaliers qualified as the No. 2 seed in the Eastern Conference playoffs. It was James' second trip to the postseason. He was helped by a coach and a roster, that season specifically, that turned out to be the best of both for that moment in his development. Under Coach Brown, the Cavaliers defended, and James was quick to buy in at that end of the floor at a younger age than most elite offensive players. He developed as a team defender alongside a collection of veterans like Ilgauskas, Gooden, Hughes, Anderson Varejao, Donyell Marshall, and others who bought in defensively as well. On the offensive end, James was allowed to do everything because he had to do everything. There were no egos—everyone was there to help LeBron. Despite aging skill sets and lack of overall depth, everyone played that role and it helped James come into his own on basketball's biggest stage.

For everything great and brilliant that Coach Brown was and still is defensively, offensive strategy was not his strong suit. To make matters worse, the team did not employ a starting caliber NBA point guard. Hughes was a starting guard in the NBA throughout most of his career, but he wasn't a point guard. Eric Snow was years removed from his glory days alongside Allen Iverson, while Damon Jones and Daniel Gibson were three-point specialists. Hughes averaged 14.9 points and 3.7 assists as the team's second best playmaker, which essentially forced James to do everything else offensively. He'd spend most of his time on that end of the floor handling the basketball, probing the defense, and freelancing to create points for himself and others while averaging 27.3 points, 6.7 rebounds, and six assists in the regular season. In order for Cleveland to win, James had to be the best player in the game every single night. On his way to his third All-Star appearance, most nights he was that.

Tim Duncan and the Spurs

People often credit Michael Jordan for never losing an NBA Finals—because of course you *should* credit Michael Jordan for never losing an NBA Finals. But LeBron played in more than one NBA Finals that his team had no business participating in—no offense intended to starting shooting guard Sasha Pavolvic, who logged 203 minutes for LeBron's Cavaliers against Chauncey Billups and Rasheed Wallace. During Game 5, for example, only Ilgauskas (16) and Daniel Gibson (11) reached doubles for Cleveland in support of 48 points from LeBron. That's with James dishing out seven assists and commanding almost all of the Pistons attention defensively. But coach Gregg Popovich and Tim Duncan's San Antonio Spurs were next level. LeBron would need more than Big Z and a banged-up Larry Hughes to get past San Antonio.

All five of Popovich's defenders seemed to have at least one foot in the paint defensively throughout each of the four games Duncan and company used to sweep King James and the upstart Cavaliers. They simply built a wall around the basket, which was anchored by Timmy, and James had nowhere to go. After the series concluded, Duncan and James were captured on video as the elder statesmen offered the 22-year-old All-Star some words of encouragement in the wake of defeat. Duncan said, "This league will belong to you one day." And Tim Duncan was right.

Chapter 9

★ ★ ★

LeBron James vs.
Wilt Chamberlain

Wilt Chamberlain
Professional Career: 1959–1973
NBA: Philadelphia & San Francisco Warriors, Philadelphia 76ers, Los Angeles Lakers
Legacy Points: 87 (No. 12)

March 2, 1962. That's when a 25-year-old Wilt Chamberlain led his Philadelphia Warriors into a matchup with the New York Knickerbockers. The contest was held in Hershey, Pennsylvania, with 4,124 fans in attendance. It was game No. 76 of the NBA season. Philadelphia would build a 79–68 lead at halftime on the strength of a dominating performance by Wilt. The seven-footer they dubbed "the Big Dipper" would have a night the basketball world would never forget, as his Warriors earned a 169–147 historic victory over New York.

The box score would later indicate that Chamberlain attempted 63 field goals that game. He'd convert 36. Wilt would also attempt 32 free throws, making 28. He dished out two assists, to go along with his daily fantasy stat line of 100 points and 25 rebounds for the contest. Chamberlain had done it—he scored 100 points in a single game.

Temple University–product Guy Rodgers led the Warriors in assists the night Wilt Chamberlain scored 100 points. Rodgers—a Philly native who played against Chamberlain's Overbrook High School Panthers—finished the game with 20 dimes. During 892 NBA career games, the 6'0" point guard who turned pro in 1958 averaged 7.8 assists. On the night Wilt scored 100, Rodgers would nearly triple that production. Al Attles (17), Paul Arizin (16), Tom Meschery (16), and Rodgers (11) would all reach double-digit points for Philadelphia while Wilt went for three.

Along the way to immortality, Chamberlain scored 23 points in the first quarter. He added 18 more in the second, heading to halftime with 41. In the third quarter, he scored 28, totaling 69 heading into the final period. He'd need to score 31 points to hit the century mark for the first time in NBA history—more than he scored in each of the three quarters preceding the fourth. But as Wilt's game wore on throughout the night, it was only his opposition who grew tired.

He'd close out with 31 to reach a single-game scoring peak that will never be threatened for the rest of basketball history. Kobe, with 81, will always remain the next closest to Wilt in single-game scoring in my opinion. And Wilt added almost 20 to Kobe's record-breaking effort to live among the clouds of NBA folklore for all eternity. The first and only player to ever score 100. But that landmark achievement was only one of the many accomplishments for Chamberlain during a star-studded career.

During that 100-point game, Wilt shot his best percentage by quarter during the second half when the game mattered most. He converted 22-of-37 field goals in the third and fourth quarter combined. He'd attempt the most free throws by quarter in the fourth (10). His rebound high came during the first quarter (10), too, before he grabbed four, six, and five to finish with 25 boards as a side note that nobody ever even mentions or seemed to notice next to the eye-popping scoring column. But when was the last time you saw someone collect 25 rebounds in an NBA game?

Wilton Norman Chamberlain, born to Olivia Johnson and William Chamberlain in 1936, always seemed to accomplish the unimaginable. He was a real life basketball superpower. Not only is there the 100-point game, Chamberlain also owns the third, fourth, and fifth highest-scoring games ever with 78, 73, and 73, against the Lakers (December 8, 1961), Chicago Packers (January 13, 1962), and New York Knicks (November 16, 1962) again. He has six games of at least 70 points on his resume, and 32 scoring at least 60.

Chamberlain and Russell

Wilt Chamberlain collected an NBA-record 55 rebounds on November 24, 1960. His Philadelphia Warriors were matched up with the great Bill Russell and the defending NBA champion Boston Celtics in Game 6 of the East Division Finals. Russell was a 25-year-old center who averaged 18.2 points and 24 rebounds during the regular season for Boston while anchoring the team defensively. Wilt was a rookie from the University of Kansas who averaged 37.6 points and 27 rebounds in his first professional season.

During the first postseason series that Chamberlain matched up against Russell in the NBA playoffs he was 23 years old. The winner of this Eastern Division Finals matchup—Philadelphia or Boston—was set to be a heavy favorite against the St. Louis Hawks in the NBA Finals. The series opened on March 16, 1960, in Boston for Game 1. Chamberlain scored 42 in his division finals debut, but Russell, Cousy and the Celtics secured a 111–105 victory. The Warriors won Game 2 by five points and Game 5 by 21 but Boston would advance to the NBA Finals in six.

Chamberlain averaged 30.5 points for the series in 1960. He did this while competing directly against an all-time legend who won his first of 11 NBA championships with the Celtics in 1957. He'd win his second in '59 and third in 1960 after eliminating the Philadelphia Warriors in an epic duel with Wilt. Over the next several years, the two icons would develop the best individual rivalry between any two NBA centers to ever play the game. "What I think about LeBron is what I used to think about Wilt," Russell told *USA Today* in 2013. "And like I told Wilt one time, 'I think I'm the only guy on the planet who really knows how good you are because I've seen you up close.'"

Dropping Dimes

Wilt Chamberlain led the NBA in scoring seven times. He led the League in field-goal percentage nine times, and rebounding 11 times. But in 1968, he also led the NBA in total assists—as a 7'1", 275-pound center for the Philadelphia 76ers.

As legend has it, Chamberlain's coach at the time, Alex Hannum, asked him to shoot less and pass more. Wilt agreed, and in 1967 he averaged 7.8 assists per game. With Chamberlain now mixing in dazzling dimes with his thunderous effort around the rim, his team got off to a 46–4 start to the season. They'd eventually eliminate the San Francisco Warriors in the NBA Finals to win Wilt's first of two championships as a player.

The next year, Chamberlain was even better, as he went on to total 702 assists to lead the League in 1968. (He also averaged 8.6 assists per game, which was second only to Oscar Robertson's 9.7.)

Rewriting Record Books

Wilt Chamberlain broke more than 70 NBA records during his 14-year professional career. He averaged 50.4 points during the season he scored 100, and totaled 31,419 for his career. The only player with more is Kareem Abdul-Jabbar, who played six more seasons. Chamberlain forced the NBA to widen the lane to 16 feet to keep him farther from the basket. Think about that. He dominated the sport of his era to such an extent that they redesigned the basketball court. He'd also be the primary reason offensive goaltending was outlawed.

Born in Philadelphia into a family of nine children. He started his college career at Kansas University in 1956 playing for the great Phog Allen. During his senior season with the Overbrook Panthers, before arriving at KU, Wilt scored 74, 78, and 90 points in three consecutive high school games. In his first varsity game for KU, Chamberlain scored 52 and grabbed 31 rebounds. He also won in the segregated city of Dallas, Texas, during the 1957 NCAA Tournament. He beat an all-white SMU team in front of a racially charged crowd that required police escorts off the court for Wilt and his African American teammates 60 years ago in a major U.S. city.

After a frustrating junior season, Chamberlain decided to turn pro. At the time, college students who entered the NBA draft before they graduated from college—or at least their senior year of free labor is completed for the NCAA—were not accepted. So, Wilt signed for $50,000 with the Harlem Globetrotters. He was in every magazine and mentioned on the nightly news in households across America. He would become known as Wilt "the Stilt" Chamberlain, the player who hit the century mark, along with a Hall of Famer. His 1967 Sixers were once voted the NBA's Greatest Team at the 35-year anniversary celebration for the NBA. He won four MVPs and two NBA championships during an unforgettable career.

Legacy of Chamberlain

The spirit of Wilt Chamberlain will live for as long as basketballs are bounced because he was that important of a player. He dared us to dream with his physical brilliance, and marvel at the way he dominated the game. He was tall and strong, but also nimble and quick. After spending most of his career in Philadelphia with the Warriors and then the Sixers, Chamberlain concluded his pro journey in Los Angeles.

From 1969 to 1973, Chamberlain wore the Purple and Gold of the Lakers. He was 32 when he arrived in LA, averaging 17.7 points and 19.2 rebounds during those five seasons. He was 36 when he retired from professional basketball. There will never be anything like him ever again. The basketball world was forever blessed by the triumphant journey of Wilton Chamberlain. He died as he lived in 1999, a towering hero among us all.

LeBron vs. Wilt Chamberlain

Legacy Power Rankings: 97 vs. 87
Chamberlain:
- **MVP award: 4 (28)**
- **NBA championship: 2 (20)**
- **NBA All-Star: 13 (39)**

LeBron will never score 100 points. Don't expect James to ever go higher than 75. That's what I'll put the career over/under for LeBron. It's probably way under, but the point is he will never be closer than that threshold to ever reaching the night Wilt Chamberlain had in Hershey. But by securing more titles than Chamberlain (the chief criticism of Wilt's career), James has already exceeded Chamberlain's total of 87 Legacy Points.

Chapter 10

★ ★ ★

LeBron James vs. Larry Bird

Larry Bird
Professional Career: 1979–1992
NBA: Boston Celtics
Legacy Points: 87 (No 11)

During a commercial break in Super Bowl XXVII, Larry Bird met Michael Jordan face-to-face for the first time—with a Big Mac on the line. In the famous ad, titled "The Showdown," the two superstars engage in a shooting competition with simple rules: if you miss, you lose.

The fellow Dream Team captains begin letting it fly from all over the court. Behind the backboard, extending out to beyond three-point range, they'd go shot-for-shot—nothing but net. The battle raged across numerous commercials, with the shots growing more and more absurd: off the scoreboard, off the rafters, to the very top of the John Hancock building in Chicago. They never missed. Years later LeBron James would remake the same commercial in homage to Bird and Jordan as a pitchman for the hamburger franchise.

Bird's Final Series

By January 31, 1993, the day "The Showdown" first aired, Larry Bird had retired from a 13-year NBA career that concluded with Gold as a leading member of USA Basketball's Dream Team in 1992. On May 17 of that year, one of the NBA's biggest icons played the last game of his professional career. His Celtics would fall 122–104 to the Cavaliers in Cleveland during the playoffs. Thirteen years after he entered the League as a college superstar from Indiana State University, Bird would hang up the hightops for good.

Cavs All-Star center Brad Daugherty led all scorers with 28 points to go along with nine rebounds and six assists in the last NBA game that Larry Bird ever played. Mark Price added 15 points and eight dimes, while John "Hot Rod" Williams came off the Cleveland bench to score 20. Bird would play 33 minutes for Boston, connect on six of nine field goals, and total 12 points on 67 percent shooting. Reggie Lewis led the Celtics with 22 points, Dee Brown came off the bench to score 18, and Kevin McHale added 15. As quickly as it all seemed to happen, it ended just the same for Larry Legend.

Bird Soaring

Bill Russell. Wilt Chamberlain. Larry Bird. Those are the only three players in NBA history since the League began issuing the MVP award in 1956 to win them in three straight seasons. Russell won in 1961, '62, and '63; Chamberlain won in 1966, '67, and '68; then Bird, in 1984, '85, and '86. Nobody else has ever done it since. Just Bill, Wilt, and Larry.

Bird averaged 24.2 points, 10.1 rebounds, and 6.6 assists on nearly 50 percent shooting from the field during the 1984 season. He had already won an NBA championship in 1981, and was in search of his second ring with Boston. Throughout the 23 postseason games, Bird improved his scoring to a playoff career high of 27.5 points per night. He'd shoot 52.4 percent from the floor, collect 11 rebounds, and lead his team to the second NBA title of a Hall of Fame career.

During the three straight years that Larry Bird was named NBA MVP, the Celtics forward logged 9,302 minutes while appearing in 241 regular season games. His three-year totals (1984–86) for points, rebounds, and assists are listed below.

Points: 6,318

Rebounds: 2,443

Assists: 1,608

That comes out to averages of 26.2 points, 10.1 rebounds, and 6.7 assists for Bird from '84 to '86, over nearly 250 games as the League's most valuable player. He'd win two NBA championships and fall just short of a third while being universally voted the world's best player. Larry was special. He, like Michael Jordan and Magic Johnson, was bigger than basketball. Bird was a transcendent figure in American sports history. He was an All-Star 12 times and an All-NBA First Team selection nine. He finished the season in the 50/40/90 club twice, making at least half of his field goals, 40 percent of his threes, and nine out of every 10 free throws. Bird was named to the NBA's 50 Year Anniversary All-Time team in 1996 and to the Hall of Fame in '98.

Celtics and Bulls Rivalry

Larry and Michael met in the NBA playoffs for the first time in 1986. The Boston Celtics were attempting to advance to the NBA Finals for the third straight season, cashing in what would hopefully be two championships in three tries. Scottie Pippen wouldn't be drafted by Jordan's Chicago Bulls until 1987. The 22-year-old shooting guard from UNC was undermanned, as a result, in his second postseason trip against the defending Eastern Conference champion Celtics.

On April 17, 1986, Bird's Celtics beat Jordan's Bulls 123–104 in Game 1 of their Eastern Conference series. Bird scored 30 on 69 percent shooting from the field, while also dishing out eight assists and grabbing six rebounds. The 6'9" sharpshooter and gifted passer was aided by 27 points and 10 rebounds from Kevin McHale, 26 from Dennis Johnson, as well as 23 and 10 from "the Chief" Robert Parish. Jordan responded with an explosive effort, scoring 49 points for Chicago in defeat.

During Game 2, MJ responded with 63. But the Celtics still won, 135–131. Bird threw in 36 points to go with 12 rebounds and eight assists to seal the victory. McHale added 27 and 15, and then the Celtics closed out the Bulls in Game 3 with an 18-point win. Jordan averaged 43.7 points, 6.3 rebounds and 5.7 assists in his first postseason matchup with Bird. Larry countered with 28.3 points, eight rebounds, and eight assists. His Celtics went on to win the NBA championship, advancing past the Bulls, Atlanta Hawks, and Milwaukee Bucks before eventually eliminating the Houston Rockets in six games for the trophy.

Bird's resume also includes Rookie of the Year honors, three All-Defensive Team awards, and three NBA three-point contest victories at All-Star weekend. Bird is essentially responsible for making the three-point contest a must-see event for basketball fans as NBA All-Star Weekend began to build mainstream momentum. Everyone wanted to see Bird after meeting the young player in the NCAA tournament in an epic 1979 showdown with fellow legend Earvin "Magic" Johnson.

Larry, Magic, and Michael brought the NBA to the mainstream for good. Each took turns ruling the NBA during the 1980s and 1990s, and Bird's dominance from '84 to '86 stands up to anyone else. He was great for more than a decade, but for those three seasons the NBA belonged to Larry Bird. Ultimately, a bad back ended his career earlier than it should have, but he was already Larry Legend. The Hick From French Lick had gone icon.

LeBron vs. Larry Bird

Legacy Power Rankings: 97 vs. 87
Bird:
- **MVP award: 3 (21)**
- **NBA championship: 3 (30)**
- **NBA All-Star: 12 (36)**

LeBron James is currently tied with Larry Bird in terms of NBA championships with three. He is also currently tied with Bird in terms of All-Star Game appearances at 12, though he's exceeded the three NBA MVP Awards that Bird won as a member of the Boston Celtics. After winning his first NBA championship for the Cleveland Cavaliers, James earned enough points (94) to move past Larry Legend on the NBA Legacy Power Rankings list.

Bird helped build an NBA brand that LeBron James would further turn into a billion dollar industry. Larry, Magic, and Michael were and forever will be paramount to the success of today's NBA. There wouldn't be the basketball theater that we see from so many talented players arriving from all over the world if it weren't for the legacy of Larry Bird, too, and his impact with the Dream Team. If his back had held out for a few more years, maybe it would've taken LeBron longer than his 13th NBA season to pass Bird on the Legacy Power Rankings list.

Chapter 11

★ ★ ★

Evolution of LeBron: Delonte West Effect

Delonte West was selected with the 24th pick in the 2004 NBA Draft by the Boston Celtics as an All-American guard from St. Joseph's University in Philadelphia. As the best local player from the Washington, D.C., area to be selected as a first round pick in the NBA in recent memory prior to Kevin Durant being selected No. 2 overall a few years later, West was a well-vetted professional prospect. Alongside Jameer Nelson, he helped Phil Martelli's team compete for a Final Four berth after leaping up the national rankings with a season-long winning streak before West declared early for the draft. West would be traded from Boston to the Seattle Supersonics before then being dealt to Cleveland. Delonte played his first game alongside LeBron on February 24, 2008, against the Memphis Grizzlies.

West quickly became not only an immediate fan favorite based on how hard he played the game of basketball, but also the best playmaker to date to play alongside James as a member of the Cavaliers. Past point guards included Jeff McInnis, Eric Snow, even Larry Hughes, who was asked to switch over from his more natural shooting guard spot, but West was an actual playmaker by trade who was coming into the prime of his career. West would help lead the Cavaliers into the 2008 playoffs still three months shy of his 25th birthday.

He proved to be a perfect complementary player alongside LeBron, especially since he was an elite on-ball defender who could also defend within the team concept. He put pressure on the opposing team's best ball-handler for the first time in LeBron's pro career, and proved to be clutch enough to support James in the scoring column during big moments. Delonte scored double-digit points in seven straight games toward the end of the 2007–08 regular season for Cleveland and appeared to be an instant steal at the trade deadline for general manager Danny Ferry's Cavs.

In 26 games as the Cavaliers starting point guard in 2008, West averaged 31 minutes for Mike Brown's Cavs while averaging 10.3 points, nearly five assists, and nearly four rebounds. In a regular season matchup with Philadelphia, West posted a double-double for Cleveland with 18 points and 11 assists. He also scored as many as 20 against his former Celtics team, and 18 again during an eight-point win that rendered the last game of the season meaningless for Cleveland. During the playoffs, West elevated his production alongside James by scoring 16 in Game 1 against Washington, 21 in Game 4, and then, most importantly, battling alongside LeBron by reaching double digits four times against Paul Pierce and the Boston team that would eventually eliminate LeBron in seven games to advance to the Eastern Conference Finals. Delonte finished with 21 points and seven assists to help Cleveland get back into the series in Game 3. He also scored 21 again in Game 5 against Boston and 15 in Game 7. But despite on-court improvement over the next two seasons, battles with mental health, racism, and a rumor-peddling society would prevent West from having the decade-long success in Cleveland it seemed he was destined to upon arrival.

Delonte West and Mental Health Awareness

Since Delonte West's professional and accomplished basketball career concluded prematurely in 2012 as a result of issues related to bipolar disorder, he has surfaced online as what appeared to be a homeless person. It's a shame that an NBA franchise or league who once employed him has been unable to reach out and successfully help Delonte overcome the issues plaguing him at this stage in his battle with mental health. According to so many metrics, West has been a remarkable success throughout his career. For a child who was born with bipolar disorder, West was able to work through those challenges that would render most

Mo Williams, LeBron, and Delonte West in the 2010 playoffs. (AP Photo/Tony Dejak)

of us helpless. He graduated from high school. He attended college. He became an All-American. He was drafted in the NBA's first round. He succeeded in the NBA. But in the end his disease got the best of him. That, and a rumor that has never been proven.

Best Supporting Actor

One of the two or three greatest individual duels of LeBron's career came in Game 7 against Pierce and the Celtics in 2008. LeBron started slow in the 2008 Eastern Conference Semifinals against Boston, scoring only 12 points in Game 1. But in Games 2, 3, and 4, he scored 21 points three straight times while posting a double-double in Game 4. In Games 5 and 6, however, James finished with 35 and 32 to set up the pivotal Game 7. Delonte had stepped in to hit big shots in support of LeBron throughout the series. West was the second best player for Cleveland during the 2008 playoff run without question. He scored over 20 against Boston twice, and in Game 7 he was the only other Cavaliers player besides James to reach double figures in scoring. Pierce totaled 41 in a head-to-head battle with James, Kevin Garnett added 13 points and 11 rebounds, while Ray Allen struggled throughout the night. After the 45 points poured in from LeBron, and 15 more from West, the next highest Cavaliers were Zydrunas Ilgauskas with eight and Sasha Pavlovic with seven.

The 2008 Cleveland Cavaliers lost the Eastern Conference Semifinals matchup with the Boston Celtics in seven games despite LeBron's greatness because the Celtics were significantly better than Cleveland from a roster standpoint. Boston lined up Paul Pierce, Kevin Garnett, Ray Allen, Rajon Rondo, and Kendrick Perkins. The Cavaliers countered with aging All-Stars Wally Szczerbiak and Ben Wallace, alongside Ilgauskas, West, and LeBron. So the Cavaliers lost the series because they were nowhere near as talented as Boston. But LeBron James was only able to be in this series because of Delonte. If not for West's production, LeBron's 40–40 duel with the great Pierce may never have played out.

Healthy and Productive

While Delonte's darkest days as a person would come during his time with the Cavaliers as his mental health issues would result in arrests where no other people were hurt or threatened, as well as to an extent rumors that were put forth with his public character or persona attached, he also excelled on and off the floor for a time in Cleveland. Delonte was a star correspondent for Jim Rome's nationally acclaimed show and also put a rap song out about Kentucky Fried Chicken and his trip through the drive through for juice and hot sauce. He is said to be an amazing artist and painter, and also an amazing teammate when healthy.

No matter where the Delonte West story goes from here—and hopefully a former team or the NBA will reach out and invest the money in him to help Delonte get healthy and clear that final hurdle in life that we all know he has the courage to clear—he will always be remembered for the way he made Cleveland fans smile as he competed with all of his heart and soul. He did everything in his power to help LeBron move closer to that first championship, and he was never afraid to fail. The rest of the world might remember Delonte for setbacks and lies that have since been associated with his narrative, but Cleveland will always keep it real with Delonte West. That's all he ever did with anyone, and that's all he ever really deserved. James and West could have been explosive together had they been able to grow at both ends of the floor as teammates. But that doesn't mean their time together as teammates will ever be forgotten by those who watched them fight alongside a city that was proud to call each player our own.

Chapter 12

★ ★ ★

First MVP

LeBron James activated 15 Legacy Points after winning his first NBA MVP award in 2009. He had made five straight trips to the All-Star Game from 2005 to '09, before being crowned the League's Most Valuable Player for the first time. LeBron averaged 28.4 points, 7.6 rebounds, and 7.2 assists on his way to earning the NBA's highest individual honor and entered the All-Time Legacy Power Rankings with 22 Legacy Points. He had led the League in scoring in 2008, after averaging his career high of 31.4 two seasons earlier. There was no longer any denying his arrival on the doorsteps of destiny. LeBron was now one of roughly 28 players in NBA history to be named the League's Most Valuable Player since first awarding the trophy in 1956.

"I'm 24 years old and I'm receiving this award, I never thought it would happen this fast," LeBron James said after receiving the 2009 MVP award. "I never dreamed about being MVP, but if I said I didn't enjoy this award I'd be lying to you. Hard work pays off and dreams do come true."

LeBron James earned 109 of the first place votes for MVP for the 2008–09 season. He totaled 1,172 points on his ballot. Kobe Bryant was next in MVP voting that year with 698 points, followed by Dwyane Wade (680), Dwight Howard (328), and Chris Paul (192) to round out the top five. Tim Duncan finished 11th in MVP voting that season after defeating James and the Cavs in the NBA Finals two season earlier, as Chicago Bulls point guard Derrick Rose won Rookie of the Year.

James had finished ninth overall in NBA MVP voting the season he won the Rookie of the Year (Kevin Garnett was named MVP that season). He finished sixth in MVP voting in his second year, and then finished in the top five from 2006 to '08 before punching through and winning the award in 2009. As a six-year pro, James had finished in the top nine of NBA MVP voting every season, and in the top five four of those six years. He'd taken over the NBA game upon arrival, and remained at the top echelon of the best players on the planet for at least 13 straight seasons.

The 2008–09 Cleveland Cavaliers steamrolled through the regular season with a record of 66–16 during LeBron's first MVP campaign. What seemed to begin as a choreographed handshake among NBA pals became nightly celebrations for a team that looked unstoppable for 82 straight games. They were fun to watch, and they were good—especially No. 23. Fan favorite Delonte West had arrived and become the best playmaker that LeBron had played with to date in his professional career. West was joined the following season by Mo Williams, who earned his only All-Star appearance of his career the year that LeBron was named League MVP. Anderson Varejao was developing into an above-average NBA power forward, and Big Z was still among the most talented offensive centers in the League. It seemed like LeBron was planning to end the championship draught that had plagued Cleveland for nearly five decades. But the closer he'd bring his franchise to their first title, the more pressure it seemed would engulf both the fan base and team.

Postseason Pressure

The youthful excitement that surrounded LeBron James' initial arrival in Cleveland had almost worn off by the time he won his first MVP. The city was starving for a ring, and the fans of Cleveland who had seen their professional teams come close but never win had already become preoccupied with constantly worrying about James' potential departure as a free agent in 2010. With five All-Star appearances, an MVP, and a fellow All-Star on the team (Mo Williams, who was added by the coaches as an injury replacement), it seemed like the ingredients were there for a potential title run. Big Z and Andy were solid enough bigs up front and Delonte had that "it" factor that championship teams always seem to have. But the lack of depth off the bench and elite playmaking around James would ultimately doom the Cavaliers.

It wasn't just Cavs fans feeling a sense of urgency based in now-or-never fear, the anxiety seemed to reverberate throughout the entire franchise. Instead of building with draft picks, for example, the Cavaliers signed whoever the biggest names were that they could get and asked Mike Brown to make it all work by playing the best defense in the League. But it didn't, not in Year Six of LeBron's professional career. After playing for Dean Smith and North Carolina out of high school, Michael Jordan needed seven NBA seasons before winning his first NBA championship, on a team where Top 50 All-Time Player and Hall of Famer Scottie Pippen was the second best player. The second best player on the 2009 Cavs was Mo Williams and it was simply not enough.

The Cavaliers opened the 2009 Playoffs by sweeping the Detroit Pistons with an average margin of victory of 15.5 points. Cleveland won Game 4 by 21 points before advancing to meet the Atlanta Hawks in the second round. James averaged 32 points against the Pistons, before scoring 34, 27, 47, and 27 in a sweep of the Hawks. Next up were Dwight Howard, Stan Van Gundy, and the Orlando Magic. Van Gundy and his staff would thoroughly out-coach their Cavs counterparts, however, while exposing the glaring weakness in the roster. Nevertheless, LeBron scored 49 points in Game 1 of the 2009 Eastern Conference Finals and dished out eight assists. But Cleveland still lost by one. James would hit a long-range bomb at the buzzer to win Game 2, and averaged 38.5 points for the series. His team, however, would fall in six games as the Magic advanced to the NBA Finals where they'd lose to Kobe Bryant's Los Angeles Lakers.

All-Around Brilliance

LeBron James finished 13th in the NBA in scoring as a rookie. He finished in third in 2005, third in 2006, and fourth in 2007, before winning the scoring title in 2008. The year LeBron won his first MVP, he finished second in scoring behind Dwyane Wade. But James has always been much more than simply an elite scorer. His basketball IQ has put him in the right position at both ends of the floor to make an impact as a rebounder throughout his career. And his court vision has always made James the best passing forward in NBA history. At a young age, his vision drew comparisons to Magic Johnson, and that would only continue throughout his career. Along with Magic, James is among the two best passers in NBA history to ever stand 6'6" or taller and continued to illustrate that point throughout his MVP campaign.

During LeBron's first five All-Star seasons, en route to his MVP in '09, he never averaged less than 6.7 rebounds per contest. He averaged 7.9 rebounds the year he led the NBA in scoring, and 7.6 heading into the Eastern Conference

Finals loss to the Magic. But even with his production on the glass and the gigantic numbers he's hung in the scoring column, it's his passing ability and vision that's separated James among the elite. As a rookie, he finished 13th in the NBA in assists for the season, ahead of both Chauncey Billups (15th) and Tony Parker (16th). He then finished sixth in assists the following year, then 12th, 15th, eighth, and ninth through 2009. His finishes at the rim were thunderous, and he seemed to elevate his game the bigger the stage, but there was something timeless about his passing. LeBron could score like Michael and pass like Magic—already—and we hadn't really seen that complete combination before from a 6'8" NBA forward who was also among the top 30 rebounders every season.

Throughout the first six years of LeBron's career, he would zip no-look passes to bigs who he seemed to throw open in the paint like Aaron Rodgers does for Jordy Nelson on a sideline out. He'd also feed West and Williams with behind-the-back dimes in transition, and Varejao up at the rim with the most precise of lob passes. There was no pass that he couldn't make, and no player he wouldn't find if the defense left him open by the rim. During the season that James won his first MVP, he dished out at least 10 assists in a game 19 times. LeBron accounted for a season-high 14 dimes in a six-point win at Portland in January on a night he also scored 34 points and grabbed seven rebounds.

LeBron would dish out 13 assists against the New Orleans Hornets in a game that Chris Paul totaled 15. He'd also pass for 13 again on a night where two-time MVP Steve Nash dished out six for his Phoenix Suns. James had effectively used a hard shoulder of all-around play to bang down the door to that elite lounge in the NBA Hall of Fame much sooner than his arrival was anticipated. But he would be met with professional adversity for the first time one year later, as basketball fans would soon announce James with boos across the country in response to a free agent decision that altered the course of professional basketball forever.

Legacy Points List: If 2009 LeBron was measured according to today's NBA Legacy Power Rankings, his 22 points would rank higher than only Derrick Rose. The former Chicago Bulls guard won the 2011 MVP award, is a three-time All-Star, and has earned a total of 16 Legacy Points. Kevin Durant was ranked directly ahead of Rose on this list before winning the 2017 championship to jump up to 41 Legacy Points.

Chapter 13

★ ★ ★

The Commercials

LeBron James has been making Scrooge McDuck money off the basketball court throughout his NBA career. Since declaring for the 2003 NBA Draft, James and his team of business associates have inked lucrative endorsement deals with brands like Nike, McDonald's, Coca-Cola, Samsung, Dunkin Donuts, Beats By Dre, State Farm, Progressive, and others. LeBron's Nike commercials, specifically, include some of his most memorable roles and performances as a pitchman. His puppet starred with Nike brand-mate Kobe Bryant's likeness in a string-pulling, season-long series. The late, great, Bernie Mac would also ask King James' congregation if he could get a layup, while "Wise LeBron" questioned real LeBron's toughness.

As a first-year pro, James starred in a Sprite *Obey Your Thirst* commercial alongside a living room full of friends that included his current agent, Richard Paul, in one of his first non-sneaker endorsements. To the chagrin of everyone in the room, the prankster, James, dupes his group into thinking he might have a career-threatening neck injury. LeBron imitates the sound of bones cracking by crinkling an empty Sprite bottle behind his head. He then reveals the trick—psych—and the room erupts in laughter. Years later, he'd help remake Jordan and Bird's iconic spot, "The Showdown." Other noteworthy stops along the YouTube deep dive through LeBron James commercials are recalled below.

LeBron's Non-Sneaker Commercials

State Farm: LeBron signs with Cleveland Browns

Every Browns fan's dream comes true in the State Farm commercial that featured LeBron James playing a unique and dominating brand of football to help Cleveland to its first Super Bowl victory in franchise history. The journey begins with LeBron at a press conference alongside two of his real-life business associates as he addresses the media from behind a well-lit podium. LeBron then introduces a No. 23 Browns jersey with his first name on the back, before taking over the NFL with mid-air field goal blocks, flying goalpost touchdown dunks, and deking approaching tacklers by bouncing the football off their helmets to create confusion. All of which ends as confetti flies in celebration of an NFL championship before James wakes up.

TNT Opening Night Promo: Show and Tell

A third grader brings his uncle into school for show and tell. That uncle happens to be a 20-year-old LeBron James who had just secured the NBA's Rookie of the Year award. Uncle LeBron arrives holding his ROY trophy and wearing his Cleveland Cavaliers uniform in this TNT spot promoting opening night for the 2004–05 season. During the question and answer period of show and tell, students ask James if he ever won a championship. They also ask the same of the playoffs. James dejectedly replies he had not, as a young woman channeling her inner-Regina George dismissively sighs and suggest her friends get back to the more important business of examining a frog. It was a tough crowd, and tough day for LeBron's nephew—whose grimace suggests disappointment with the lack of professional accomplishments.

McDonald's: LeBron Monopoly Commercial

LeBron would work with McDonald's from 2010 to 2014. After investing in a competing restaurant chain upon his return to the Cleveland Cavaliers, James and Ronald McDonald's iconic hamburger brand would mutually agree to part ways. But during their run together, James appeared in successful marketing campaigns like "The Showdown" reboot of the legendary Jordan and Bird shooting competition, as well as the restaurant's monopoly game promotion. In one of those monopoly spots, the big voice guy compares the chance for customers to win prizes with LeBron's chances of passing Jordan in the championship ring department by securing seven. James smiles and shrugs, plays along with the joke, and even peels off a chance for free fries as he prepared to crush a Big Mac. LeBron and the fast food brand would part ways while James listed two titles and four MVPs on his professional resume, totaling 78 Legacy Points compared to MJ's 137.

ESPN SportsCenter: Where's My Chair?

LeBron starred opposite longtime ESPN personality Scott Van Pelt in a SportsCenter commercial that debuted on the network in 2007. The cubicles for both Van Pelt and King James shared a common divider. We learn this when LeBron arrives back at his desk and is instantly perplexed to find a standard office chair in the place his throne usually rests. The King politely asks Scott, who appears to be draped in a fur blanket, if he has any idea what happened to his chair? Van Pelt claims he does not, while sitting in an extravagantly large and comfortable red seat. James is forced to slump down in a spartan office chair, and bang out Excel documents just like the rest of us except for the NBA uniform he was wearing.

Beats By Dre: RE-ESTABLISHED

The two-minute-and-32-second extended version of the Beats By Dre commercial, "RE-ESTABLISHED," was released on October 18, 2014, as LeBron James was embarking on the first season of his return to Northeast Ohio as the leader once again of the Cleveland Cavaliers. The YouTube description that accompanied this powerful video included the following as constructed by the headphone maker: "The words 'Akron Est. 1984' are inked on LeBron James' body. Moving back to Cleveland in 2014 is the re-establishment of his legacy in Northern Ohio. He now embarks on the next and greatest chapter of his career." The touching film opens as Gloria James uses her own words to welcome her son back home to Ohio, as we first see him entering the doors of Akron St. Vincent– St. Mary High School, while James uses Powerbeats2 Wireless headphones to prepare for a run of championships in Cleveland.

LeBron's Nike Commercials

Nike: Chalk Toss

Nike released LeBron's "Chalk Toss" commercial in celebration of his arrival among basketball's elite the same year he won his first MVP award. This tribute features the Cleveland Cavaliers superstar's unique and signature pregame chalk toss ritual. As chalk dust flies from basketball courts to barbershops throughout the story, we're met with a series of courtside cameos provided by recording artist Lil Wayne without context. In his final appearance, as LeBron now has the entire arena chalk tossing during an NBA game, Wayne can be seen brushing that dust off his shoe. A high-flying slam by the player that Nike invested in before he entered the League signals the end.

LBJ Signature Shoe Era: Around the time this commercial debuted, James was promoting the Air Max LeBron VIIs. This installment of LeBron's signature sneaker was among the first designs to use Nike's Air Max cushioning system in a basketball shoe.

Nike: LeBron, Kobe, and the MVP Puppets

LeBron continues chalk tossing in puppet form early on in his legendary Nike series, co-starring the likeness of Kobe Bryant and others. LeBron's puppet is wearing a Cavaliers uniform while tossing chalk all over a condo he shares with the NBA's elder statesman, Bryant. He is celebrating his first trip to the postseason as a member of the Cleveland Cavaliers, which occurred in 2006.

During 13 playoff games that season, LeBron averaged 30.8 points and 8.1 rebounds. Kobe, meanwhile, had won three NBA championships by the time his puppet was introduced alongside James. Bryant would go on to win an MVP shortly after, before LeBron secured his first in either category. This classic series featured LeBron's puppet wearing a headband and squeezing out over 2,000 curls. He's also eating cereal and hanging in a barbershop when Zydrunas Ilgauskas arrives. The former All-Star and center for the Cleveland Cavaliers and later Miami Heat pops his puppet head in with some DVDs for sale. The two friends exchange choreographed handshake routines like they do during games on the sidelines from there.

LBJ Signature Shoe Era: Around the time this commercial debuted, Nike was promoting the LeBron 8. This sneaker once again featured the Air Max system with an updated location for the swoosh logo, pushed more toward the heel than in previous releases.

Nike: The LeBrons

The "LeBrons" were a Nike commercial series that featured a Wise, Business, and Kid version of LeBron along with his real life version over two seasons. The debut of this series was arguably the first time that James demonstrated at least serviceable if not solid acting skills. Nike said in their press release announcing the second season of The LeBrons: "The personalities are reflective of the depth and dimension of the young James, the sole actor in each spot. Wise is an old-school old-soul living in an environment of youth and hyperactivity. Business is cool, calculating, and highly confident. Kid displays the joyful exuberance of a child, while the athlete LeBron James embodies superior physical attributes and talent." The "Pool" episode would open the second season, as Wise LeBron scoffs at real LeBron's decision to work out in a training pool. "You can't get through Detroit training in a pool," the older character says. "Do you think Michael trained in a pool?"

Signature Shoe Era: During the time The "LeBrons" aired, James was promoting Nike's Zoom LeBron III and IV. The shoes represented the third and fourth installment of James signature line and first series to use his name in the name of the shoe.

Nike: Training Day with John Legend

The Training Day commercial was among the most prominent campaigns to which James would first attach his "Strive For Greatness" slogan or hashtag. The commercial with John Legend singing down from the heavens is both stoic and inspirational. James goes on to lead a bike tour through the city's streets, as Akron's children join him in a massive bicycle parade through the city. In Rocky Balboa fashion, the neighborhood kids are inspired by James and his bicycling expertise and hop on their 10-speeds to bike toward greatness. As the camera pans away at the close of the video, it seems to foreshadow the images captured forever years later as the Cavs championship parade flooded Cleveland's streets once again.

Signature Shoe Era: The LeBron 11 was released around the time James led this bike tour through Akron with John Legend singing as the city collectively peddled forward toward greatness. The LeBron 11 was called the lightest LeBron shoe constructed to date.

Nike: Together

This commercial was both timelessly constructed as well as perfect for its moment. As the announcers bellow the upcoming return of Cleveland's hometown star for the first time, on the day the 2014 NBA season was about to begin, James is seen taking the floor in a Cavaliers uniform. Nike athlete Kyrie Irving is the first teammate featured alongside James. Anderson Varejao, Tristan Thompson, and Dion Waiters also make appearances. As James encourages his team to bring home a championship for Cleveland, the fans of Northeast Ohio walk to the floor in support of the team. LeBron's high school coach, Dru Joyce II, makes a cameo, The LeBron James Family Foundation bus filled with kids drives by, as the city of Cleveland unites once again in support of their Cavaliers. James also speaks like a young Vince Lombardi on his goal to help his team become their very best.

Signature Shoe Era: Released upon the start of LeBron's first season back in Cleveland, Nike used the Together campaign to help sell the LeBron 12. They certainly sold more pairs of the 12s in Cleveland than they had over the previous few seasons.

Chapter 14

★ ★ ★

LeBron vs. Shaquille O'Neal

Professional Career: 1992–2011
NBA: Orlando Magic, Los Angeles Lakers, Miami Heat, Phoenix Suns, Cleveland Cavaliers, Boston Celtics
Legacy Points: 92 (No. 10)

On October 26, 1993, the reigning NBA Rookie of the Year was preparing for his second season with the Orlando Magic. As a 20-year-old, first-year player, selected No. 1 overall out of LSU, Shaquille O'Neal dominated the League upon arrival. Appearing in 81 regular season matchups as a rookie, he averaged 23.4 points, 13.9 rebounds, and 3.5 blocks. His sophomore campaign, as the fastest-rising pro athlete in America, would tip off in roughly one week. That's when *Shaq Diesel* was released by Jive Records.

Shaq Diesel was a hip-hop album by Shaquille O'Neal featuring production from legendary musicians like Ali Shaheed Muhammad of A Tribe Called Quest. The track Ali produced with Shaq, titled "Where Ya At," also included a guest appearance from ATCQ's trendy gladiator, the late, great MC Phife Dawg. Other albums that Jive released that year included Tribe's *Midnight Mauraders* project. Two years earlier, Jive also dropped *Homebase* by DJ Jazzy Jeff and the Fresh Prince, along with many other notable albums.

Shaq's full-length rap project produced by a label with some of the biggest acts in the industry featured musical collaborations with Def Jef, Erick Sermon, and Fu-Schnickens, among other producers and lyricists. Packaged with an album cover featuring Shaq's face, seemingly hologrammed off the galaxy sky, and his full name in Magic Blue across the top, Shaq Diesel would reach as high as No. 25 on the Billboard List before eventually being certified platinum. On and off the floor, Shaq was a megastar.

Platinum Status

Alongside a young, supremely talented guard in Anfernee "Penny" Hardaway—who would become, before injuries, an All-NBA player on an annual basis—the Magic rolled into Miami for the first game of O'Neal's second season for a matchup with Rony Seikaly's Heat. Shaq went for 42 and 12, and the Magic won 116–96. About three months later, by the morning of March 20, 1994, the Magic awoke with a chance to win their 40th game of the season. But despite 29 and 16 from Shaq, they'd stumble against the Lakers. The next day, *Shaq Diesel* was certified platinum for selling one million copies.

Shaq and Penny's Magic would eventually earn a berth in the Eastern Conference playoffs the year Shaq's lyrical skills were certified platinum as everything the young player seemed to touch turned to gold both on and off the floor. Meanwhile, the first radio release for Shaq Diesel, titled "(I Know I Got) Skillz" made it to No. 35 on the Billboard Hot 100 List. The second single, "I'm Outstanding," made it to No. 47. A guest appearance by Shaquille on the Fu-Schnickens hit, "What's Up Doc? (Can We Rock)," was also certified gold during the regular season as well—only year two for a young superstar known simply as Shaq.

Shaq's Playoff Debut

The Indiana Pacers were led by a 28-year-old shooting guard named Reggie Miller in 1994. They would meet Orlando for the Eastern Conference quarterfinals. Miller knocked down two three-pointers during Game 1 on his way to 24 points. The two-time All-Star from Orlando matched Reggie with 24 points of his own, to go along with a game-high 19 rebounds. Shaq's Magic led 26–20 as the first quarter concluded.

Shaq and LeBron as teammates in 2010. (AP Photo/Tony Dejak, File)

There were only two other Pacers who managed to score double-digit points on the night in support of their Hall of Famer. Orlando, meanwhile, saw starters Nick Anderson, Dennis Scott, and Penny Hardaway all reach double figures, surrounding Shaq as starters, while Donald Royal came off the bench to also score 14. But the veteran Pacers were determined to secure the postseason victory.

The Magic built a 54–42 advantage at halftime, but after cutting the lead to eight points heading into the fourth quarter, 74–66, the Pacers came from behind for the win 89–88. They led the Magic 1–0 as O'Neal searched for the first postseason win of his career in Game 2. Unfortunately for Magic Nation, he'd wait much longer than that for his first taste of postseason success.

Shaq, Jordan and the Dream

Shaquille O'Neal would not win his first postseason game until April of the following year, after being eliminated by the Indiana Pacers in 1994. On April 28, 1995, however, they'd be back in the first round squaring off against Dee Brown, Dominique Wilkins, and the Boston Celtics. The Magic won Game 1 by 47 points as Orlando secured the series in four games. The Chicago Bulls, led by Michael Jordan and Scottie Pippen, were next.

Shaq averaged at least 29 points during the regular season for the second-straight time while also grabbing 11.4 rebounds. Along the way, he won the 1995 NBA scoring title and appeared in his third All-Star Game. He would now match up with the great Jordan and Pippen, alongside his youthful partner named Penny.

His Airness had retired and been gone for the entire 1993-94 season and the majority of the '94–95 season, having recently returned to the NBA by the time he first met Shaq in the playoffs.

During Game 1, on May 7, 1995, Jordan led the Bulls in scoring with 19 points. Shaq, meanwhile, led all scorers and rebounders with 26 and 12, while four other Magic teammates scored at least 14 points. The Eastern Conference semifinals were tied 43–43 at the break. Nick Anderson connected on 3-of-6 three-pointers to finish with 20 in support of O'Neal for the Magic. Hardaway led Orlando in assists with six to complement 16 points of his own. Horace Grant (a three-time champion as Jordan and Pippen's former teammate) added 16 as well for the Magic, to go along with seven rebounds. They built a four-point lead after three quarters before eventually securing the win, 94–91.

The Magic and Bulls drew even at 2–2 heading into a pivotal Game 5. Michael dropped 39 points on 54 percent shooting while also grabbing four rebounds. B.J. Armstrong added 18 points, while Pippen paced the Bulls in rebounding with 11. But Shaquille was simply unstoppable. The Big Fella scored 23 points and collected 22 rebounds to lead his team to a 3–2 series advantage over Chicago.

Dennis Scott hit five threes to finish with 22 points in the Game 6 victory, while Penny flashed a 19-point, 11-assist double-double. He combined with O'Neal for 42 points, 27 rebounds, 15 assists, and six blocks in the contest. Their legendary counterparts—Jordan and Pippen—combined for 49, 15, seven, and four. The Eastern Conference Finals were up next.

The Pacers had made short work of Orlando during Shaq's first trip to the postseason. They ended his young Disney adventure in three straight games. But this was an improved, and now experienced team the Pacers were facing when the Magic returned for revenge in Game 1. Shaq would lead all scorers in response to a Hall of Famer–caliber effort from Miller. The Big Aristotle tossed in 32 while grabbing 11 rebounds. Penny finished with 20 points and 14 assists. The Magic built a 35–21 third quarter advantage to eventually erase a five-point halftime deficit, en route to a 105–101 victory.

On June 4, for Game 7 of the ECF, Shaq and Penny were back at home after the Magic lost by 27 in Game 6 in Indiana. During what was the biggest game of the young franchise center's career to date, he answered the bell with 25 points and 11 rebounds in Game 7. The Magic won, and were now going to the NBA Finals. Shaq would finish the 1995 playoffs with postseason averages of 25.7 points and 11.9 rebounds over 21 games. He shot 58 percent from the floor, dished out 3.3 assists, and recorded nearly two blocks per night. He would meet the most skilled interior center in the League at that time, Hakeem "the Dream" Olajuwon, and the Houston Rockets for the NBA Finals—and young Shaquille would lose.

Shaq's NBA Reign

In 2000, Shaq led the Los Angeles Lakers to the first of three straight NBA championships. He'd add a fourth ring in 2006 as the starting center for the Miami Heat, a team paced by a young Dwyane Wade. O'Neal would average 18.4 points and 9.8 rebounds for Miami during 23 postseason games. His championship pedigree, engaging swag, and relevant talent made it easy to see the decisive victory coming. But during his three-peat run in LA, the League revolved around O'Neal.

Miami would not have won the 2006 NBA championship without Dwyane Wade. But they also wouldn't have won that year without Shaq. Just as Kobe would not have won his first three without O'Neal. He was the biggest star on the planet. He represented a new world order from the center position. He was music, movies, endorsement deals, and Hollywood. He was Los Angeles. But he was also basketball at its rawest and strongest and most violent around the rim.

Shaq tore down basketball hoops during NBA games and lifted spirits afterward by offering a thesaurus of nicknames and witty responses to post-game reporters. He was funny, creative, talented, and unique. He was the best NBA center I've ever seen play during my lifetime. He was simply invincible at his very best.

LeBron vs. Shaquille O'Neal

Legacy Power Rankings: 97 vs. 92

O'Neal:

- **MVP award: 1 (7)**
- **NBA championship: 4 (40)**
- **NBA All-Star: 15 (45)**

When you isolate the fact that Shaq and Kobe won three straight NBA championships from 2000 to '02, and then consider they only earned one League MVP combined during that stretch, it might become more possible to understand why the two young superstars might have felt like feuding for more of the national spotlight during their time as teammates together. But like Kobe, Shaq only earned one MVP, compared to at least four for LeBron. These MVP awards helped James move just past O'Neal and into the Top 10 at No. 9 heading into the 2018 season with 97 Legacy Points. This is despite trailing the Big Aristotle by one NBA championship, and three All-Star Game appearances.

Chapter 15

★ ★ ★

Evolution of LeBron: Zydrunas Ilgauskas Effect

LeBron's relationship with Zydrunas Ilgauskas is unique because it spans essentially all of James' life as a high-profile basketball player. As a young prodigy in Akron, the Cleveland Cavaliers coach at the time, John Lucas, invited James to practice with the local NBA team. When he eventually did, the Cavs best player at the time was Zydrunas Ilgauskas. The team was later fined by the League for having an amateur involved in a professional practice. But the invite from Lucas would result in one of the first times that LeBron ever got onto the basketball court with Zydrunas Ilgauskas. Big Z would play for Cleveland from 1997 to 2010, spending seven years as LeBron's teammate with the Cavs before concluding his career in Miami after James joined the Heat.

Ilgauskas was an All-Star center in the Eastern Conference during LeBron's senior year at Akron SVSM. He would also earn a trip to the All-Star Game as James' teammate in 2005, and eventually help LeBron lead Cleveland to an Eastern Conference championship in 2007. While he'd play in Miami for the 2010–11 campaign before calling it a career, Zydrunas would never earn an NBA championship ring. But that did not stop LeBron from doing everything he could to help get Ilgauskas there. All the while, Big Z would marry a girl from Cleveland and start a family in the area. He'd give back consistently and become an all-time great Cleveland sports icon as a result of his performance, attitude, and personality. In these ways, Ilgauskas would serve as James' first professional role model and help him learn about life as a professional outside of the game. From an inside-out standpoint, Z would also help James create space and force defenses to respect the interior with an underrated offensive game which was ahead of his time in many ways from the versatile, skilled style of center who dominates the game today.

In the Cavaliers starting center, LeBron had a legitimate co-star from the standpoint of competing on a nightly basis during the regular season for a playoff spot. But it would take several midseason trades and roster overhauls to eventually put enough talent around LeBron and Big Z for the run in the postseason. That would not occur until their fourth season together in 2007, as James and Ilgauskas led Cleveland past Chauncey Billups, Rasheed Wallace, and the Detroit Pistons before falling to Tim Duncan and the San Antonio Spurs. Big Z battled serious injuries throughout his professional career, but during the 2006–07 campaign he appeared in 78 games alongside LeBron, averaging 12 points and eight rebounds per contest. During the Cavs postseason run, which was highlighted by one of LeBron's greatest all-time games (Game 5 at Detroit), Ilgauskas upped those contributes to 12.6 points and 9.7 rebounds. During the 2007 Playoffs in support of LeBron, Big Z scored at least 20 points three different times. He also collected 18 rebounds in Game 3 against the Spurs and also grabbed 19 rebounds in Game 4 against Washington. Ilgauskas was a teammate that LeBron knew he could trust, and was the first person that James ran to hug after his team eliminated the Pistons to advance to the NBA Finals.

LeBron and Big Z's Jersey Retirement

There was never a debate about whether or not Zydrunas Ilgauskas was going to get his jersey retired by the Cleveland Cavaliers franchise from essentially the point in 2007 when he helped LeBron advance to the Finals through his final game of the 2009–10 season. But when LeBron James left for Miami, fan favorite for over a decade and a personality that was considered to be as Northeast Ohio as it gets, the Lithuanian sensation who arrived in Cleveland in the mid-90s would announce he was leaving for Miami too.

Zydrunas Ilgauskas, Dwyane Wade, and LeBron share a laugh on the bench during the fourth quarter of a 2010 game against the Nets. (Howard Smith-USA TODAY Sports)

It makes sense when you step back without the emotion of Cavaliers fans at that moment and ask why would Ilgauskas not want to play what he expects to be his final season for a team that now employs all of the best players? But it was still tough for Cavs fans to swallow, so there was some talk about whether or not to retire his jersey after the 2011 season but not all that much. This was until the Big Z jersey retirement ceremony was put on the schedule during the 2014 season.

In March 2014, I published the following on my Cavs Blog, StepienRules. com, in anticipation of Big Z's jersey ceremony. My story was quickly cited by *The Cleveland Plain Dealer* later that day and thrown into the national news cycle. I was told that LeBron was planning to return to Quicken Loans Arena to attend Ilgauskas' jersey retirement ceremony and published the following.

March 2, 2014, via StepienRules.com:

I keep hearing that LeBron James will be attending Zydrunas Ilgauskas' jersey retirement ceremony on March 8 at Quicken Loans Arena. So much so that I felt obligated to write about it.

According to multiple sources I've spoken with, there is a very good chance that James will be attending the Cavaliers game against the New York Knicks on Saturday to show support for his longtime teammate and friend. It is not believed that James will have any role in the ceremony, but there is an expectation that he'll be in the building as Ilgauskas' No. 11 jersey is raised to the rafters.

James played with Ilgauskas as a member of the Cavaliers from 2003 to '10. They then spent the 2010–11 season together as members of the Miami Heat. Some of Z's most celebrated moments obviously include James as a result.

It's hard to look back at Ilgauskas' career and not remember, for example, James running to hug Big Z first in celebration of the Cavaliers winning the 2007 Eastern Conference championship. It's also difficult to simply dismiss the outstanding performance of Z's likeness as a DVD salesman in LeBron's Nike puppet campaign.

The Miami Heat are scheduled to play in San Antonio on Thursday, March 6. They are off on Friday and Saturday before playing in Chicago on Sunday.

If James actually does make a stop in Cleveland this weekend, it will be interesting to see how that's received by Cavs fans. There could be a contingent of fans who appreciate James paying homage to a Cavaliers' legend like Z who is universally loved and celebrated on the night his jersey is being retired. There could also be other fans who are upset to find out that he's there.

The report I published was later confirmed by LeBron James and his camp. The Miami Heat superstar would eventually attend the jersey retirement ceremony for Big Z. He would sit in Dan Gilbert's box and walk through the back hallways of Quicken Loans Arena without being verbally attacked by fans like he was in his first, second, and third games back to compete against the Cavs. This night celebrating Ilgauskas as a Cleveland Cavalier would set the stage for LeBron's return later that summer. This public mending of relationships between owner, organization, and fans was a healing moment, as the No. 11 made famous in Cleveland by the center forever known as Big Z was lifted to the rafters.

Working Through Injuries

Maybe one day we'll learn all of the specific things that LeBron learned from Zydrunas. Maybe it involved banking or investment tips, or eating tips, or how to pack for road trips, or how to prepare during off days, when to show up to practice, or maybe those bonds they shared went even deeper. But what James did learn at an early age by observing or being around Zydrunas was how to work through injuries and prepare your body to avoid injuries as much as possible. LeBron saw Ilgauskas miss time due to foot and ankle issues. He watched him as a fan in high school as he battled through a series of devastating injuries to eventually develop seven years after being drafted into an All-Star. Maybe watching Big Z go through all that helped impact how LeBron would build the body-training regimen that has kept him healthy and effective throughout his entire career.

What if Zydrunas Ilgauskas was a player that never got hurt? What if LeBron watched him make that All-Star game in 2003 without knowing he overcame significant injuries to get to that place? What if Big Z hadn't helped fight back in time to be an All-Star when LeBron made his first trip in 2005? Or what if Big Z quit fighting and playing before the 2007 playoffs? His career arc will be forever marred by injuries but those who spent time around Big Z always knew he never stopped working. Because LeBron has never stopped working on his body off the court since first becoming teammates with Z, he's also never missed significant time. He learned by watching Z how precious this game is, how unique of a chance the world's greatest players have to play it. He learned lessons that helped him become LeBron James because of the fact that he crossed paths early on with a seven-foot Lithuanian named Zydrunas. No matter how many times he got hurt or whatever changes from this moment on, it will always be impossible to adequately tell the LeBron James story without at least mentioning his longtime teammate named Z.

Chapter 16

★ ★ ★

Back-to-Back MVPs

"I'm sorry," James said as he stood in front of about 3,000 fans at the University of Akron's Rhodes Arena accepting his second-straight MVP award. "I've got to have my teammates up here with me, man. There's a lot of credit to the people who help me along the line. I need those 14 other guys who put up with me and I put up with them."

As good as it all seemed to be that day, the climate for the Cavaliers in Cleveland would change dramatically as soon as the season ended.

LeBron James tore off his NBA best-selling Cleveland Cavaliers No. 23 jersey in frustration as he walked to the locker room at Quicken Loans Arena following a Game 6 Eastern Conference semifinal loss to the Boston Celtics that eliminated Cleveland from the playoffs. The 25-year-old unrestricted free agent from Akron, Ohio, who won the League MVP award for the second straight time during the regular season was no longer officially a member of his hometown Cavs. Gordon Gund won the 2003 NBA Lottery for the chance to select LeBron No. 1 overall seven years earlier. Dan Gilbert bought the franchise because a young James was on it. But change was on the horizon, and that didn't feel good for Cavs fans.

As the NBA universe courted the six-time All-Star and two-time MVP in hopes that he would earn their franchise millions of dollars and win an NBA championship, the Northeast Ohio community waited. LeBron and his professional representatives were meeting with basketball delegates from the Los Angeles Lakers, New York Knicks, Miami Heat, Brooklyn Nets, and anyone else who could talk their way into a sit-down of any duration. The case was presented of how franchises like those led by Hall of Famers like Pat Riley or Jerry West could help LeBron acquire the Legacy Points needed to enter the conversation with players like Michael Jordan (137 Legacy Points) and Kobe Bryant (111 Legacy Points) by winning championship rings. Through seven seasons in Cleveland, James played in six All-Star games (18 Legacy Points) and won two NBA MVP awards (14 Legacy Points) for a total of 32 Legacy Points. But he needed to start stacking titles, and he'd team up with Dwyane Wade and Chris Bosh in Miami to do specifically that.

When LeBron eventually announced—live, on ESPN, in the aptly titled *The Decision*—that he was signing with the Heat, the reaction from Northeast Ohio fans was devastation. Dan Gilbert played to that emotion with the scorched-earth letter he posted in response, in which he called LeBron's exit a "cowardly betrayal" and guaranteed the Cavaliers would win a title before LeBron James ever did. (Later, when LeBron was considering returning to Cleveland, Gilbert and he would talk about the letter, with Gilbert apologizing for it and LeBron apologizing for his handling of *The Decision*.)

LRMR in Downtown Cleveland

The founders of the marketing brand LRMR each have their name represented in the brand's name: LeBron James, Randy Mims, Maverick Carter, and Richard Paul. This company has led to the launch and success of many local brands, companies, musicians, and others throughout the Northeast Ohio area to this very day. It would also eventually lead to Klutch Sports, the sports agency headlined by Richard Paul with support from longtime NBA agent and local Northeast Ohio legend Mark Termini. Springhill Entertainment, the Hollywood arm of LeBron's modern day empire, can also trace roots to LRMR, who hosted *The Decision*, the most highly covered media spectacle in NBA free agent history, during the summer of 2010.

LRMR occupied corporate office space in downtown Cleveland not far from the headquarters for legendary sports agent IMG. In that office space near East 9th Street in downtown Cleveland, the LRMR team, along with LeBron's CAA player agency representatives, met with the NBA elite. Hollywood-caliber paparazzi captured pictures that would appear in newspapers all over America of James and his entourage in cars driving to and from meetings. The Cavs made a video with fart jokes according to legend, and Coach Riley dropped his rings on the table. LeBron went in search of Legacy Points, and stunned the NBA world by selecting the Miami Heat as his next professional adventure.

Chapter 17

★ ★ ★

LeBron James vs. Bob Cousy

Bob Cousy
Professional Career: 1950–1963, 1970
NBA: Boston Celtics, Cincinnati Royals
Legacy Points: 106 (No. 9)

Robert Joseph Cousy was known as "The Houdini of the Hardwood." He led the NBA with an innovative style of playmaking, whipping passes like Jason Williams nearly three decades before the former Kings point guard was even born. Cousy's up-tempo, anticipatory style of running the Boston Celtics offense from the point left basketball fans and defenders collectively stunned. He invented the modern day assist, essentially, if not also inspiring the direction offensive basketball would continue to move to over the next 60 years.

Cousy played a plodding, two-handed set-shot sport much quicker than anyone ever had before. He was moving faster, but also thinking faster. He was playing chess on the NBA hardwood in a game driven by checkers-caliber strategy. Along the way, Bob Cousy raised six championship banners for the Boston Celtics while appearing in 13 All-Star Games and winning the 1957 NBA MVP with averages of 20.6 points and 7.5 assists.

The Cooz inspired fans to pay hard-earned money in the 1950s to watch him pass the basketball. They weren't paying to see him dunk it. They weren't even paying to watch him shoot. Bob Cousy made the pass cool for one of the very first times in pro basketball history. In doing so, he also helped put people in seats with a court vision never before witnessed in an exploding sport that James Naismith invented 59 years before the Celtics drafted the most iconic point guard in franchise history. Cousy would dish out a career-high 9.5 assists during the 59–60 campaign while also scoring 19.4. During his second season in the NBA, he topped out at 21.7 points. The 1951 rookie sensation from Holy Cross would retire in 1963 with career averages of 18.5 and 7.6. As a 40-year-old coach for the Cincinnati Royals later in 1970, Cousy played a few dozen games as part of a ticket-sales campaign before hanging it up for good.

Cousy was in his sixth NBA season when his Boston franchise coached by the great Red Auerbach drafted a rookie named Bill Russell. The League's all-time winningest player would inspire innovation and change on the defensive end of the floor by leaping to block opposing player's shots early on in his career. This defied coaching logic of the day that recommended defenders keep their feet on the floor so they wouldn't get juked by an opposing ball-handler. The point guard and center tandem, Cousy and Russell, moved offensive and defensive basketball forward together as Boston teammates for the next decade.

The Celtics point guard won the second MVP in NBA history in 1957. Bob Petit won the first in '56 with the St. Louis Hawks. His Celtics would win their first NBA championship in franchise history that same year. Boston would then rip off an eight-peat from 1959–66. Cousy would play his last game for the Celtics in 1963, before a packed house at the Boston Garden to announce his retirement. The son of poor French immigrants, Cousy was described as a "ghetto rat" growing up in the slums of Manhattan in the late 1930s. His college coach benched him early in his career for "showboating" and limited his minutes in response to his creative passing. But Bob Cousy would continue to express himself, altering the course of basketball history with an innovative approach to the sport he loved.

Boston Tear Party

Cousy held his retirement ceremony on March 17, 1963, in front of a sell-out crowd at Boston Garden. United States president John F. Kennedy wired to

Cousy in response to the news: *"The game bears an indelible stamp of your rare skills and competitive daring."* The crowd had just watched Cousy help the C's to their sixth championship, averaging 13.2 points and 6.8 assists as a 34-year-old guard who appeared in 76 regular season games. But now he was hanging it up—as the Boston faithful looked down at their great hero in despair from the seats inside the arena as he addressed the crowd.

The *Boston Globe* looked back at the 50-year anniversary of this announcement:

"At the event, soon to be dubbed 'The Boston Tear Party,' a weeping 34-year-old Cousy read from handwritten remarks, his vocal cords slowly tightening, his voice choked to a whisper, and for one brief moment Cousy and the sellout Garden crowd lapsed into almost pin-drop silence. Until...

"'We love ya, Cooz!'

"The shout came from the old barn's upper reaches, bellowed by Joe Dillon, a water department employee from South Boston. It provided the signature moment to a storybook day, and Cousy remains ever grateful for the assist, Dillon's words the serendipitous distraction that allowed him to escape his own emotional full-court press. The crowd erupted. Cousy took a deep breath and continued."

Cousy would eventually deliver his message to fans and be handed keys to a Fleetwood Cadillac, as he rode off to that place where legends go when their brilliance leaves the sport in physical form. He forever will be Boston royalty and an NBA pioneer, an artist who saw the race at a different speed. The note that President Kennedy wired to Cousy was printed on the game programs distributed to fans the night of his announcement.

Assisting an Era

More than 50 years after he retired from NBA basketball, Cousy's assist totals are still holding up. The game would only get quicker over the decades following his retirement, but Cousy's dimes have kept pace. He is currently five places behind LeBron James on the all-time NBA assists list with 6,955, which is good for top 20 all-time. During his MVP season in 1956–57, Cousy led the NBA in total assists with 478, which was 111 assists more the next closest player. He also averaged 7.5 assists that year, which was nearly 2.5 more than anyone else, either, on a nightly basis. The year before Cousy turned pro, Dick McGuire of the New York Knicks led the League with 386 dimes. Cousy was pushing the tempo and inspiring his contemporaries to do the same, while dishing out roughly 100 more assists than McGuire. The station-to-station style of play that prevailed throughout the sport before Cousy would be changed forever because of him.

Nightmares of a Legend

In Bill Reynolds book, *Cousy: His Life, Career and Birth of Big Basketball,* he describes the challenges that the Celtics legend faced on his rise from being born poor to immigrant parents and considered a "Ghetto Rat" to retiring on St. Patrick's Day in Boston in front of a packed Garden crowd who yells out that they love him to break the tension when words become too difficult to muster. Cousy understood how much those fans wanted to win and he cared about those feelings. He also knew how important an expression of sport had quickly become to so many people across the NBA landscape.

In Reynolds' book, this was illustrated beautifully.

"He was one of the first basketball players to do endorsements, one of the first to have his own basketball camp. He enjoyed the kind of celebrity that was unheard of for a basketball player of his era, often being called 'Mr. Basketball.' But he had a price to pay for that.

"For years [Cousy] had nightmares. Bill Sharman, who roomed with him on the road for 10 years, used to say that it was not uncommon to wake up in the middle of the night and see Cousy walking around the hotel room speaking in French, although he hadn't spoken in French since his childhood. As his career progressed, these episodes had become more common.

"These nightmares eventually became so upsetting, so bizarre, complete with running out of his house and going down a road, that he'd gone to a psychiatrist, who told him he was having anxiety attacks and gave him medication for them. By the end of his career, he had developed a nervous tick under his right eye, a physical manifestation from the pressure he felt."

Despite that pressure, the childhood poverty, and a battle with mental health issues during an era when understanding and support for such issues was almost non-existent, Cousy delivered. He delivered as a champion for his friends, family, and fans of the Boston Celtics. And every pass you never saw leave his hands changed this great game of basketball. He was the Cooz, and everybody loved him.

LeBron vs. Bob Cousy

Legacy Power Rankings: 97 vs. 106

Cousy:

- **MVP award: 1 (7)**
- **NBA championship: 6 (60)**
- **NBA All-Star: 13 (39)**

LeBron James has not yet passed Bob Cousy on the Legacy Points Power Rankings prior to launching his 14th NBA season. He would need to win three more championships to match Cousy's total of rings. But LeBron does have three more MVP awards, which gives him a chance to sneak past the Houdini of the Hardwood over the next couple seasons. If James never wins another championship or MVP he will pass Cousy with five more All-Star appearances to total 18 before his NBA career concludes.

Chapter 18

★ ★ ★

First Title

The biggest competitive mistake LeBron James made as a pro to date was attempting to embrace the villain role thrust upon him for the way he made his decision to leave Cleveland and sign with the Heat. For everything that LeBron always was, playing the role of the heel was something that never came natural. He'd struggle with this persona while attempting to develop chemistry with his new superstar teammates, Dwyane Wade and Chris Bosh. Eventually it all came together, as they went on to win multiple championships. But in their first season together, the 2011 Heat would ultimately advance to the NBA Finals before being extinguished by Dirk Nowitzki and his Dallas Mavericks.

The "Mavaliers" was a regretful term used by scorned Cavaliers fans who rooted hard for the Mavericks in the 2011 Finals. At that point, those fans from hater-ville headquarters in Cleveland were pulling for whomever could keep LeBron from winning a title. "Cavs for Mavs" was another witty phrase and hashtag that was tossed around social media in the early takeover of Twitter. LeBron did not anticipate that type of response when he made his free agent decision. Nobody really did. Not in 2009 and 2010, while a young James was winning 60-plus games for the Cavs and multiple League MVP awards.

But it did happen, and now the professional sports world was tuned in around the clock to see how LeBron and his new teammates would respond. The Miami Big Three combined for 65 points and 28 rebounds in a Game 1 victory before finding themselves down 3–2 after a 29-point effort from Nowitzki, heading into

Game 6 of the 2011 NBA Finals. James, Wade, and Bosh each scored at least 17 points in the closeout game, while combining for 20 rebounds, but it wasn't enough. Mark Cuban's Mavericks would use 21 more from Dirk and 27 from Jason Terry to secure the NBA championship.

Combining the alpha dog scoring personalities of players like LeBron James, Dwyane Wade, and Chris Bosh—three superstars who entered the League as the first, fourth, and fifth players selected overall in arguably the greatest draft in history—would take more time than people anticipated. It would take time for Bosh—as an example—to find his most efficient scoring opportunities while playing alongside his ball-dominant All-NBA teammates. Making the transition from a franchise player with the Toronto Raptors, who every play was designed for, to learning how to be able to play off James and Wade, was a significantly underrated individual challenge for Bosh that required time and mental toughness to overcome. The question about whose team the Miami Heat belonged to, in terms of who was the biggest of all these alpha dogs—Wade or James—and who would be tasked with the hypothetical role of "always taking the last shot" circled the Heat locker room as well. But eventually, three of the top 25 basketball players on planet Earth figured out how to not only play together, but to win big together.

2012 NBA Finals

The 2012 NBA Finals matchup between the Miami Heat and Oklahoma City Thunder seemed to offer promise of potentially becoming a modern-day version of the Celtics vs. Lakers. LeBron James was 27 years old with three MVPs by the time he met a pair of 23-year-old first ballot Hall of Famers in Kevin Durant and Russell Westbrook. James Harden was coming off the OKC bench during the 2012 NBA Finals as a 22-year-old offensive assassin, too, while a 27-year-old Bosh looked for his first ring as a 30-year-old Wade went for ring No. 2. LeBron averaged 28.6 points, 10.2 rebounds, and 7.4 assists during the NBA Finals while wining his first championship in a five-game elimination of OKC. "As much as I loved my teammates back in Cleveland, and as much as I loved home," James said on his way to defeating Kevin Durant, Russell Westbrook, and James Harden in the 2011 NBA Finals, "I knew I couldn't do it by myself against that team. I apologize for the way it happened, but I knew that this opportunity was once in a lifetime."

LeBron won his third MVP award in his second season with the Heat. He'd also make his eighth All-Star game and win the NBA championship while being named Finals MVP. James, Wade, and Bosh had proven to be the League's best three teammates, as well as the best team. Despite a more than commendable Finals effort from Durant and Westbrook, who averaged 30.6 points and six rebounds and 27, 6.4, and 6.6, respectively, Miami made short work of the young Thunder.

To close out Game 5, LeBron put his signature stamp on his first championship with a 26-point, 13-assist, 11-rebound triple-double. Wade added 20 points and eight rebounds while Bosh totaled 24 and seven as the Heat won 121–106. Miller came off the bench as the Heat sixth man to knock down 7-of-8 three-pointers during Game 5 to finish with 23 points and five rebounds. Battier (11 points) and Chalmers (10 points) each reached double figures for Miami. Durant led OKC with 32 points and 11 rebounds in Game 5, meanwhile, as Westbrook and Harden each added 19.

LeBron in Wade County

The NBA culture and measuring stick personified by Michael Jordan's Bulls, Isiah Thomas' Pistons, Larry Bird's Celtics, or Magic Johnson's Lakers, that ultimately suggests an All-Star also needs a successful franchise that is singularly his—a thinking that drove Shaquille O'Neal and Kobe Bryant away from each other as co-starring, all-time great players in Los Angeles—was something that threatened all members of the Big Three from earning the true value of championship-caliber Legacy Points according to critics. Was this a team that belonged to LeBron or Wade? Who deserved to take the last shot? These were some of the outside voices or criticisms that continued to storm the shores of South Beach during the early months of the Big Three. There were also questions that LeBron James would eventually answer on the basketball court by earning the MVP award during the regular season and NBA Finals while securing his first title. He was still the best player in the world and he was now finally on the best team.

During the regular season, all three members of Miami's newly minted Big Three were named to the 2012 Eastern Conference All-Star team. Later, in the NBA Finals against Durant, Westbrook, Harden and the Thunder, LeBron would score 32, 29, 26 and 26 to win Games No. 2–5. Wade and Bosh also put up huge numbers in the series, with Wade scoring 24, 25, 25 and 20 in respond to the opening loss of the series. Bosh finished with scoring nights of 16 points, 10, 13, and 24, along with an 11-rebound effort during that same stretch. The NBA's greatest free-agent superstar experiment had resulted in two trips to the NBA Finals and one championship during its first two seasons of ruling the NBA Kingdom from Miami.

Moving Up the Legacy Power Rankings

During seven years with the Cleveland Cavaliers—an era that began in a season where LeBron James finished No. 9 in the NBA MVP voting while also winning Rookie of the Year—James totaled 32 Legacy Points. Those Legacy Point totals with the Cavs break down as follows:

- 6 All-Star Games (18 Legacy Points)
- 2 NBA MVP Awards (14 Legacy Points)

During his first two seasons in Miami, James added the following:

- 2011 NBA All-Star (3 Legacy Points)
- 2012 NBA All-Star (3 Legacy Points)
- 2012 NBA MVP (7 Legacy Points)
- 2012 NBA champion (10 Legacy Points)
- Total: 23 Legacy Points

By earning 23 Legacy Points in only two seasons, James would total 55 through his first nine years in the NBA. He'd win another championship and MVP during his 10th professional campaign in 2013, along with making his ninth trip to the All-Star Game for 20 more Legacy Points. That would then give him—by the summer of 2013—a total of 43 Legacy Points earned in three years with Miami, for a total of 75. If LeBron James finished his career after nine seasons with those 75 Legacy Points, he would rank directly behind Wilt Chamberlain and Larry Bird, who each retired with 87 Legacy Points. Michael Jordan retired with 137. Directly behind James would be Moses Malone with 70.

James would need some combination of four more All-Star appearances (12 Potential Legacy Points) or one more title (10 Potential Legacy Points) or MVP (7 Potential Legacy Points) to make up the 12-point gap between that repre-sents the No. 13 spot overall. This would take at least two if not three or four seasons.

LeBron hugs Dwyane Wade in the final moments of their 121–106 win over the Thunder in Game 5 of the NBA Finals. (AP Photo/Lynne Sladky, File)

James averaged 26.7 points, 7.5 rebounds, and 7.0 assists in his first season with Miami. He improved that scoring output to 27.1 during his first championship campaign in 2012. LeBron would also improve his shooting percentage from 51 percent in 2011 to 53 percent in 2012, while accounting for 7.9 rebounds and 6.2 assists. After critics suggested that James would be forced to take a back seat to Wade in the scoring column when he first joined Miami, LeBron continued to lead his team in each of the major statistical categories on most nights. This efficient dominance would only continue for the newly crowned champion during his quest to repeat in 2013.

LeBron Wins Third MVP

LeBron James finished with 1,074 points in the NBA MVP voting to win his third trophy in 2012. During his first MVP with the Heat, James finished just ahead of Kevin Durant, who totaled 889 MVP points. Chris Paul, the 26-year-old Los Angeles Clippers point guard and close friend of LeBron's, finished third in MVP voting that season, while a 33-year-old Kobe Bryant was fourth, and Tony Parker came in fifth. Finishing No. 6 was Minnesota Timberwolves big man Kevin Love, a future teammate of LeBron's in Cleveland, and finishing No. 10 in MVP voting that year was his current teammate, Dwyane Wade. Dwight Howard—who McDonald's would pair with James in their Super Bowl Big Mac commercial remake of the Jordan and Bird classic—finished No. 7, Rajon Rondo No. 8, Steve Nash No. 9, and 35-year-old Tim Duncan No. 14.

LeBron finished second in total field goals made while winning his third MVP award with 621 on the season. Kevin Durant finished first with 643 field goals made for the Thunder. James led the League in two-point field goals made with 567 (Los Angeles's Blake Griffin was No. 2 with 559), and player efficiency rating at 30.7 (LAC's Chris Paul was second at 27). He became more efficient in order to help create additional scoring opportunities for Dwyane Wade, Chris Bosh, and others throughout the Heat roster. James would also lead the NBA in average plus/minus rating, finishing one of the greatest seasons in NBA history with an average of +11 points per game plus/minus while on the court during the year (Chris Paul finished second in this category at 7.9).

Chapter 19

★ ★ ★

LeBron and Hip-Hop

"I always think back to the Jay-Z phrase and a line he had," LeBron James said during his postgame press conference after a Cleveland Cavaliers Game 3 loss to the Toronto Raptors in the 2016 Eastern Conference Finals. Questioning his reason for not retaliating to hard fouls in kind, James used a line from Jay-Z's *Friend or Foe* project. He explains, "If I shoot you, then I'm brainless. If you shoot me, you famous. What am I to do?"

The NBA universe wasn't watching to see the Raptors punish James with hard fouls and physical play. They were watching to see how he'd respond. If LeBron earns a Flagrant 2 in response to a hard foul by Toronto, he knows his judgment, as a team leader, will be questioned. Some might even say he's brainless for getting suspended. But instead of sounding defensive, he just offers us Hov. As a guest on Scott Van Pelt's late night *SportsCenter* weeks later after clinching the NBA title, he'd make a similar analogy—only this time he'd reference a song.

"I just go back to the Jay-Z song 'A Star is Born,'" James told Van Pelt while wearing an NBA championship hat and waving an unlit cigar like Red Auerbach from the Cavaliers locker room. "You guys back in the studio go look it up, listen to it. I just always listen to that and I always stay true to the game. I know what I'm capable of not only on the floor, but also off the floor as well—with my leadership and what I bring to the table."

LEBRON JAMES VS. THE NBA

"A Star is Born" was released on Jay-Z's *Blueprint 3* album and features an up-and-coming J.Cole. Jay-Z lists a number of successful rappers throughout the song who emerged to essentially claim, or compete for, Rap MVP status at various points of his music career. While praising those platinum-selling runs of artists like Wu-Tang Clan, Mobb Deep, T.I., Kanye West and Eminem, among others, Jay-Z is essentially arguing that he was at least an All-Star caliber MC or better during each of those eras, spanning from DMX in the early 2000s to Lil Wayne, and then Drake.

This consistent longevity among the elite, Jay suggests, helps support his argument of being the greatest rapper of all-time. As LeBron carried his team back from 3–1 to beat Stephen Curry and the Golden State Warriors after their recording-setting season, this song was something James would go back to. In a league filled with young talent and emerging Hall of Famers like Curry, Kevin Durant, Russell Westbrook, James Harden, and many others, LeBron is still winning championships in triumphant fashion well past his 30th birthday. Just like Jay-Z and each new wave of great rappers, James is still holding down the No. 1 spot in his profession as well—despite the many stars born into the NBA everyday.

Kurtis Blow's Basketball

Hip-hop pioneer Kurtis Blow released one of rap's first ever professionally recorded albums. He is largely considered the first commercially successful rapper to sign with a major record label. In 1980, Blow, aka Kurt Walker, released a single from his debut album called *The Breaks*. It would become rap's first record to be certified gold. In 1984, Kurtis Blow released his fifth studio album, titled *Ego Trip*. That record's single, "Basketball," would also be recognized on the Billboard charts. It was released the same year Larry Bird won the first of his three straight MVP awards while leading the Celtics to a championship. One year after this song was recorded, Michael Jordan won NBA Rookie of the Year honors and LeBron James celebrated his first birthday.

Hip-hop and basketball were intertwined long before LeBron joined SVP on ESPN following his third NBA championship. The musical sound born in New York during the same time that Kareem Abdul-Jabbar and Fly Williams were dominating the city's playgrounds has always been interconnected. Professional athletes, like James, are among the many people who not only dance and enjoy hip-hop music, but also find inspiration and meaning in its message. Similarly, rappers like Blow and the thousands who followed continue to find inspiration in the NBA's best as well.

Kurtis Blow, for example, specifically mentions the names of 23 players in his 1984 classic, "Basketball." His opening verse is as follows:

Basketball is my favorite sport,
I like the way they dribble up and down the court,
Just like I'm the King on the microphone, so is Dr. J and Moses Malone,
I like Slam-dunks, take me to the hoop,
My favorite play is the alley-oop,
I like the pick-and-roll, I like the give-and-go,
Cause it's Basketball, uh, Mister Kurtis Blow

Along with NBA MVPs Julius Erving and Moses Malone, the rap icon also goes on to shout out Wilt Chamberlain, Magic Johnson, Larry Bird, Kareem Abdul-Jabbar, and Bill Russell. He calls Kareem the center on his starting team, and also mentions Wilt's 100-point game and Russell's Celtics championships. Since then, rappers would continue to reference the NBA's best over the next three decades and beyond.

Kanye West and *The Decision*

Kanye West is among the many notable rappers who have used LeBron's name on a record as a noun, verb, adjective or status symbol synonymous with being the best. One of West's better LBJ name-drops came on a feature from a Jadakiss track, "Gettin' It In" released in 2004—the same year that LeBron would win NBA Rookie of the Year honors. The second was recorded on Kanye's "New God Flow" track in 2012, after James won his first NBA championship with the Miami Heat. Those two lines are as follows:

"Gettin' It In" (2004)

"Trying to figure out since Kan' came. Who the rookie of the year, me or LeBron James?"

"New God Flow" (2012)

"From the most hated to the champion God flow. I guess that's a feeling only me and LeBron know."

LeBron was considered the most hated among NBA fans at the time because of the way that he left the Cleveland Cavaliers. While Cavs fans may have been angered by the sheer fact that he did leave their team to join the Miami Heat, LeBron's image or reputation took its biggest dent as a celebrity because of how he left. Specifically, after courting several NBA teams at high-profile meetings in downtown Cleveland all summer, James made the legendary announcement of taking his talents to Miami to join Dwyane Wade, Chris Bosh, and the Heat on an ESPN primetime special billed as *The Decision*.

While the NBA world tuned in to see which team the sport's greatest player was going to be playing for next season, we were met with LeBron, host Jim Gray, and seated in front of the stage among a handful of chairs at a Boys and Girls Club fundraising event in 2010 was Kanye West. Legend has it, Kanye was hitching a ride with James and company on a private jet that was scheduled to take them to Carmelo Anthony's wedding after the announcement. For that reason, potentially, he put his mark on the NBA's highest profile free agent signing event of all-time. One former Rookie of the Year watching another change the course of basketball history forever.

Jay-Z Courtside at McDonald's Game in Cleveland

The Cleveland Cavaliers averaged 11,946 fans per game during the 2002–03 season. As a college student at nearby Case Western Reserve University that season, I don't recall purchasing a ticket all year. But I did buy a ticket to the 2003 McDonald's All-American Game at Gund Arena to watch Northeast Ohio superstar LeBron James measure his skills against the best high school basketball players in America. When we sat down in our seats in the upper bowl, Jay-Z was seated courtside directly in our line of sight. He was the biggest celebrity I had ever seen or recalled watching a game in Cleveland in my life at that time.

Chris Paul, Luol Deng, and Kendrick Perkins were among the future NBA stars who competed alongside James that night. LeBron finished with 27 points, while future Cavs teammate and longtime NBA veteran Shannon Brown scored 23. CP3 finished with a game-high 10 assists, but it was LeBron who had Jay-Z and everyone else in the arena on their feet all night long. He was a prodigy on his way to taking over the NBA universe, and every fan left certain of this singular fact: LeBron James was a superstar. In every sense of the word, unlike any other high school superstar to ever come before him, LeBron was a superstar. He had talent, hype, he was packing arenas, outselling the Cavs, and putting every game he played in on the national marquee. It was different, it was special, and it was only the beginning.

More Than a Game Soundtrack

LeBron arrived at Akron Civic Theatre in Akron, Ohio, in the summer of 2009 for the premier of the critically acclaimed documentary, *More Than a Game*, which chronicled his high school career. He'd arrive with good friend and former McDonald's All-American Chris Paul among others for the screening. Alongside a crowd of media, friends, family, teammates, and others, the premier of this documentary played out to a receptively engaged audience. The hip-hop soundtrack that accompanied this film would also feature some of the most successful rappers in the music business.

The first single released from this soundtrack, which peaked as high as No. 8 on the Billboard charts in 2009, was titled "Forever." The song included verses from Drake, Eminem, Kanye West, and Lil Wayne. During a stoppage in a Cavaliers game that season, the camera zoomed in on LeBron who was singing along to this song word-for-word as it blared through the Quicken Loans Arena speakers. This soundtrack, celebrating LeBron's high school journey, also included rappers T.I. and Jay-Z, along with the Queen of hip-hop, Mary J. Blige.

Chapter 20

★ ★ ★

LeBron James vs. Julius Erving

Julius "Dr. J" Erving
Professional Career: 1971–1987
ABA: Virginia Squires, New York Nets
NBA: Philadelphia 76ers
Legacy Points: 106 (No. 8)

Julius Winfield Erving II finished the 1978–79 campaign strong. The 28-year-old small forward for the Philadelphia 76ers wrapped up his third NBA season with averages of 23.1 points, 7.2 rebounds, and 4.6 assists. It marked his eighth straight professional season averaging at least 20 points, 6.5 rebounds, and 3.5 assists. After two years with the Virginia Squires, and three more with the New York Nets—both of the ABA—Erving had officially become a mainstream star. Both on the court and off, everybody in America knew Dr. J.

During that same year, David Dashev and Gary Stromberg co-wrote a movie that opened to a theatrical release named *The Fish That Saved Pittsburgh.* Loosely inspired by the ABA spirit of teams like the Squires or Nets, the story features a fictional basketball franchise that was down on its luck for many reasons. But they find a way to preserve through teamwork and believing in one another as their franchise player, Moses Guthrie, leads the way with the help of a young team manager.

While playing their home games at the Pittsburgh Civic Arena, the Pythons break training camp with a lineup that simply doesn't gel. But the basketball hero played by Erving in the movie saves the season. In the role of Guthrie, Erving turns in a nuanced and brilliant performance that makes the light-hearted basketball film a cult treasure. He is always cool, always inspiring, yet inviting and reachable. Just as he dared us all to be with every step he took on the basketball court.

An NBA Star Arrives

During his first three years with the Philadelphia 76ers, Erving would cross paths with some of the biggest names in the history of basketball. His teammates included Doug Collins, Daryl Dawkins, George McGinnis, Mike Dunleavy, Maurice Cheeks, and others when he first arrived from the ABA. His head coach was Billy Cunningham, and among the Philly assistants was the great Chuck Daly. Later, he'd pair with Hall of Famer Moses Malone and win an NBA championship.

Erving's Sixers played their home games at the Spectrum in Philadelphia. He was tall and strong, yet also seemed to slowly float through the air on his way to the basket at his own speed. He played above the rim, but he did so with a graceful elegance that was unique. He inspired others to elevate around him, and he'd change the way basketball was played along the way, in the rim-pounding style that Michael Jordan—and later LeBron James—would accelerate.

"He played in an era where he was basically ahead of his time," James told NBA.com. "The athletic ability, to do the things he did on the floor was never seen before. He was faster than anybody else, athletically. From my eyes, it didn't seem like anyone was at his level. He was ahead of his time."

Playoffs and Championships

Julius Erving advanced to the playoffs during each of the 11 seasons he played in the NBA. He'd appear in 141 NBA postseason games for his career, and then another 48 postseason contests in the ABA. During those NBA playoff games for the Sixers he averaged 21.9 points, 7.0 rebounds, and 4.2 assists.

As a rookie in Philadelphia, Erving led his team to the NBA Finals, where they'd lose in six games to the great Bill Walton and his Portland Trail Blazers. Julius averaged 30.3 points during the series. Dr. J would also lead Philadelphia back to the NBA Finals in 1980 and 1982, losing to Kareem Abdul-Jabbar and the Los Angeles Lakers in each of those next two trips. In 1983, however, the Sixers would break through to become champions after aligning Erving's talent with free agent Moses Malone. Erving won two ABA titles in 1974 and 1976, as well, and then finally defeated the defending NBA champion Los Angeles Lakers to win his first in the Association and third overall.

During the four-game sweep of the Lakers in 1983, Dr. J averaged 19 points per contest. His Sixers would win a decisive Game 3 by 17 points and go on to sweep in Game 4 with a seven-point victory. In the final game, Moses Malone scored 24 points and grabbed 23 rebounds. Andrew Toney—the eighth overall pick in the 1980 draft—tossed in 23 for Philadelphia, while Erving scored 21. Maurice Cheeks finished with 20 points and seven assists.

How Dr. J Got His Nickname

Julius Erving credits a high school friend named Leon Saunders for being the first person to ever call him Doctor. Julius called Leon "the Professor" when they were kids. Leon called Julius "the Doctor." As the Roosevelt High product in New York City rose to prominence, the crowds gathered at the historic Rucker Park basketball courts to watch a young prodigy the fans first glossed "Black Moses." But Erving would instead insist, politely, that if you were to call him anything other than his real name, don't call him "Black Moses," call him "the Doctor."

In 1968, Dr. J enrolled at the University of Massachusetts. During two seasons of work, he averaged 26.3 points and 20.2 rebounds. He would leave school early to pursue a professional career, but not be eligible for the NBA draft until 1972. Although he'd later be selected 12th overall by the Milwaukee Bucks, Erving would begin his professional career in the ABA. He'd eventually negotiate a contract with the Virginia Squires upon his departure from UMass.

Erving would lead his team to the East Division Finals as a rookie with the Squires, before falling to Rick Barry and the New York Nets for a berth in the ABA Finals. The New York City native averaged 27.3 points during his rookie season. He would continue to dominate for the next four years, winning championships and scoring titles while doing everything he could to keep the upstart basketball league in business. It was a stretch of brilliance on the hardwood that inspired legendary sportswriter Terry Pluto to call Erving, "the greatest player in ABA history," in his critically acclaimed book *Loose Balls*.

Legendary Status

Erving retired from basketball in 1987 at the age of 36. He won four MVP awards and three championships as a professional. He was named to both the NBA and ABA All-Time teams, and inspired a generation of players who followed him to jump higher, finish stronger, and play smoother than they ever might have without him. He was must-see television on the basketball court. He was Moses Guthrie on the silver screen. He was Black Moses at the Rucker. He was Julius "Dr. J" Erving in the pages of basketball history—the coolest basketball icon to ever live.

LeBron vs. Julius Erving

Legacy Power Rankings: 97 vs. 106
Erving:

- **MVP award: 4 (28)**
- **NBA championship: 3 (30)**
- **NBA All-Star: 16 (48)**

Julius Erving currently has nine more Legacy Points than LeBron James has earned through 2017. He beats James exclusively in terms of All-Star game appearances. He has played in three more than LeBron through the first 13 seasons of James' career. James matched Erving's championship total by winning his third in 2016 as a member of the Cleveland Cavaliers and making the All-Star game that year to earn 13 Legacy Points for a total of 94. If James doesn't get there, he's expected to make at least three more All-Star games to tie Erving and then eventually pass him on the Legacy Power Rankings before retirement.

Chapter 21

★ ★ ★

Evolution of LeBron: Dwyane Wade Effect

LeBron James and Dwyane Wade were two of the NBA's three best players during the 2009–10 season. In 2006, Wade, teamed with Shaquille O'Neal, delivered Miami its first of three championships as a member of the Heat. They even changed the county name to Miami-Wade County for a week in 2010, that place exploded each time his Jordan's touched the hardwood. Outside of winning his first ring, some of Wade's most notable matchups came against fellow Class of 2003 superstar LeBron James and his Cleveland Cavaliers. Wade's duels with LeBron are maybe only eclipsed by Paul Pierce's individual run at James during the 2008 playoffs especially. An argument can certainly be made for LeBron's regular season battles with Kobe Bryant as well, but there was no denying the anticipation among NBA fans when Wade and James would collide.

When LeBron joined the Miami Heat during the summer of 2010, his merger with Wade represented two of the NBA's best players overall playing now for the same team. The stats and the narratives almost seem to make us forget soon after an era concludes, but Wade was top three without question in 2010. During each of the four seasons he played with James, he was basically top five. Would you have really taken five guys before Wade in 2012? Who are they? Because LeBron and Wade ended up playing like two of the League's best three players were now on the same team. They dominated.

It took one more season than people expected, but they would eventually take over. What was missed as they launched their mission along with Bosh, however, was that they weren't getting clutcher, getting more alpha or living bigger in a big moment. What they launched was the mission to build the best team around their collective talent as possible. That took one season finishing as the NBA's runner up. Then they ripped off two straight while leaving no question as the NBA's two best teammates since Michael Jordan and Scottie Pippen.

The fact that calling an NBA superstar a Scottie Pippen type is an insult is one of the many glaring examples of how our sports dialogue today can be embarrassing. People think that being the second best is admitting to being a loser, I guess? But the truth was, Jordan was the best players on his championship Bulls teams. Scottie Pippen was the second best. It was Jordan's team, he was most alpha. But Pippen is a top 40 NBA all-time player at worst, so really what you are saying is you have a top three and top 40 all-time player on the same team in MJ and Pippen. The Miami Heat, similarly, had a top three all-time player in LeBron James and a top 40 all-time player in Wade. This is not who they were when James arrived on the shores of South Beach. But the top 50 all-time player wing of the basketball's immortal Hall of Fame will always belong to the greatest player that LeBron ever called his teammate—the iconic Dwyane Wade.

James vs. Wade

Basketball Reference's Head2Head matchup tool at BasketballReference.com generated a result of 29 matchups between LeBron James and Dwyane Wade through the 2017 NBA All-Star game. During those 29 games, LeBron has won 15 times and Dwyane has won 14. LeBron's first matchup with his fellow rookie, Wade, came on November 12, 2003. James scored 18 and Wade totaled 14 while also securing the victory. Later that season, the two friends and former teammates in Miami would each score at least 20 points for the first time. Wade got the win while pouring in 20 points as James countered with 24. Just before Christmas in 2005, they each exceeded 30 in the same game for the first time. LeBron went for 41 as Wade countered with 33 to combine for over 70. In a 2006 matchup between the Heat and Cavs, James and Wade each went over 40.

They'd each go over 40 again in 2009, all the while contributing in all areas of the game as they have become known to do.

LeBron's top 20 scoring games while competing against Dwyane Wade as a member of the Cavaliers are listed below via Basketball Reference. Five of these 20 games through the 2017 NBA All-Star Game have come after James and Wade were teammates in Miami. Two of those five games also come in matchups against Wade and the Chicago Bulls, who he joined prior to the 2016–17 campaign. The legend of this rivalry, however, was written in the many duels between two of the NBA's best teammates before they joined forces in legendary fashion.

1	James (CLE)	3/12/2006	Wade (MIA)	47
2	James (CLE)	4/1/2006	Wade (MIA)	47
3	James (CLE)	3/2/2009	Wade (MIA)	42
4	James (CLE)	12/17/2005	Wade (MIA)	41
5	James (CLE)	12/30/2008	Wade (MIA)	38
6	James (CLE)	2/4/2010	Wade (MIA)	36
7	James (CLE)	11/12/2009	Wade (MIA)	34
8	James (CLE)	12/28/2008	Wade (MIA)	33
9	James (CLE)	1/25/2010	Wade (MIA)	32
10	James (CLE)	2/3/2005	Wade (MIA)	31
11	James (CLE)	1/4/2017	Wade (CHI)	31
12	James (CLE)	12/25/2014	Wade (MIA)	30
13	James (CLE)	2/2/2006	Wade (MIA)	29
14	James (CLE)	2/9/2007	Wade (MIA)	29
15	James (CLE)	10/30/2015	Wade (MIA)	29
16	James (CLE)	1/21/2008	Wade (MIA)	28
17	James (CLE)	1/28/2004	Wade (MIA)	27
18	James (CLE)	12/2/2016	Wade (CHI)	27
19	James (CLE)	3/16/2015	Wade (MIA)	26
20	James (CLE)	3/19/2016	Wade (MIA)	26

The top 20 scoring efforts of Dwyane Wade's career during games he competed against LeBron James and the Cleveland Cavaliers (pre-and post-Heatles

Days) are listed below. Wade exceeded the 40-point mark four times during his career matchups with James. While LeBron reached a higher overall total (47), he eclipsed the 40-point mark as many times as his friend Dwyane in the series. But regardless of how many they scored and which team earned the victory, every NBA fan who had the chance was watching LeBron take the floor with the kid from Marquette who was balling in Miami.

1	Wade (MIA)	4/1/2006	James (CLE)	44
2	Wade (MIA)	1/21/2008	James (CLE)	42
3	Wade (MIA)	2/1/2007	James (CLE)	41
4	Wade (MIA)	3/2/2009	James (CLE)	41
5	Wade (MIA)	11/12/2009	James (CLE)	36
6	Wade (MIA)	3/12/2006	James (CLE)	35
7	Wade (MIA)	12/17/2005	James (CLE)	33
8	Wade (MIA)	1/25/2010	James (CLE)	32
9	Wade (MIA)	3/16/2015	James (CLE)	32
10	Wade (MIA)	12/25/2014	James (CLE)	31
11	Wade (MIA)	12/28/2008	James (CLE)	29
12	Wade (MIA)	11/4/2004	James (CLE)	28
13	Wade (MIA)	2/9/2007	James (CLE)	27
14	Wade (MIA)	3/7/2009	James (CLE)	25
15	Wade (MIA)	10/30/2015	James (CLE)	25
16	Wade (MIA)	2/2/2006	James (CLE)	24
17	Wade (MIA)	2/4/2010	James (CLE)	24
18	Wade (MIA)	3/19/2016	James (CLE)	24
19	Wade (CHI)	12/2/2016	James (CLE)	24
20	Wade (MIA)	12/25/2007	James (CLE)	22

The low-hanging fruit, gotcha news cycle that we all seem to chuckle, sneer, and sometimes even cheer, will lead us to believe through a series of rapid fire takes on sports platforms of traditional and digital media that LeBron and Dwyane and Bosh choked in 2011. They somehow played to less of who they were as players, because—as the narrative went—they were finally embarrassed for dancing like egotistical rich punks at that announcement party. Now they realize how wrong

Heat Big Three fan event. (AP Photo/J.Pat Carter)

they were for doing that, I guess, and we supposedly watched them place the ball on the ground and give up against the Dallas Mavericks. But it is a lifelong lesson of teamwork we miss when we do this while glossing over educational aspects of the Big Three soap opera we all hoped would transpire, I guess, when LeBron, Bosh, and Wade tipped it off on Day One.

What ultimately made the pairing of LeBron James and Dwyane Wade is the same thing that made the pairing of Michael Jordan and Scottie Pippen before them successful. It was also the same thing that made Magic and Kareem ultimately successful for as long as they were, and the same thing that helped Moses Malone and Julius Erving team up as former MVPs to win a ring together.

Best since Mike and Scottie

Shaq and Kobe are different than Mike and Scottie. O'Neal is a center, and the nature of a center makes the dynamic duo conversation inherently different if it's compared to perimeter contemporaries. That's a long way of saying that Shaq and

Kobe was more Kareem and Magic than Michael and Scottie. Jordan and Pippen, as two wings offensively, compare more directly to LeBron and Dwyane. And in saying as much, there was not two better teammates anywhere else in the NBA than Wade and James since each player entered the League.

They threw full-court alley oops to each other. They left high-flying finishes dangling for each other to dispose through the rim with regularity. They led *SportsCenter* almost every night. They each forced the opposition to tip their defense, and it proved impossible to guard both LeBron and Dwyane when they were each at their very best. Not that it ever was possible before they teamed up in the first place. Playing alongside LeBron for four seasons in Miami, Wade averaged 26, 22, 21, and 19 points per game. He helped his friend win two more MVPs and his first two titles. It's impossible to write the LeBron James story without measuring the impact both on and off the floor of his great friend from the 2003 NBA combine.

Chapter 22

★ ★ ★

Back-to-Back Titles with Heat

LeBron James made the third NBA Finals appearance of his career while winning his first ring in 2012. In 2013, he'd appear in his fourth Finals and third straight with the Heat. This string of dominance would extend for (at least) seven seasons (counting the 2017 NBA Finals). The Heat won the Eastern Conference every year from 2011 to '14 and then the Cavs won in '15, '16, and '17, for seven consecutive Finals appearances for LeBron as a player, along with a 2007 Eastern Conference title with the Cavs for eight career Finals appearances. The GOAT, Michael Jordan, played in six NBA Finals, winning rings in each appearance.

Jordan appeared in his first NBA Finals series in 1991 against the Los Angeles Lakers. He averaged 31.2 points, 11.4 assists, and 6.6 rebounds on 56 percent shooting from the floor while eliminating Los Angeles in five games. MJ was 27 years old. LeBron was 22 years old (five years younger than Jordan) when he appeared in his first NBA Finals. By the time LeBron was 27, he was appearing in his third NBA Finals. James lost two NBA Finals before Jordan ever appeared in one, and they both won their first ring at age 27.

A 28-year-old LeBron James would defend his first NBA championship and third MVP award during the 2012–13 campaign with 26.8 points, 8.0 rebounds, and 7.3 assists on his way back to the NBA Finals for a third straight time and fourth overall. James would also shoot a staggering 56.5 percent from the floor overall while putting up these numbers, along with a career-best 40.6 percent from three-point range. The kid who entered the League without a jumper was not only winning championships and MVPs, he was also improving his game. The biggest weakness that LeBron James possessed when his professional career began was his three-point shooting. He was now over 40 percent from deep as a 6'8" forward—on the season—who was still rebounding like a monster and leading his team in assists.

D-Wade averaged 21 points, five rebounds, and five assists while the Heat began to defend their NBA championship during the 2012–13 regular season. Bosh averaged 17 and seven, Mario Chalmers was coming into his own as a steady player, and the great Ray Allen had been added to the lineup. The all-time great sniper shot 42 percent from three during the regular season for Miami, while averaging double-digit points in 79 games as a 37-year-old from UConn wrapping up a Hall of Famer career with championship class. Shane Battier, Cleveland State University's Norris Cole, Udonis Haslem, Mike Miller, Chris "Birdman" Andersen, Joel Anthony, Juwan Howard, James Jones, and others all continued to play key roles in the championship rotation for Miami. They won 66 games and opened against the Milwaukee Bucks in the playoffs.

2013 NBA Playoffs

LeBron James, Dwyane Wade, Chris Bosh, and the Miami Heat opened the 2013 NBA playoffs against Brandon Jennings, Monta Ellis and the No. 8 Milwaukee Bucks. The Heat won four straight games by no less than 11 points. They beat the Bucks by 23, 12, 13, and 11. Next up was the Chicago Bulls, who sent a wake-up call to Miami with a 93–86 victory in Game 1. But James, Wade, Bosh, Allen, Cole, and Chalmers each scored at least 11 points, as The King went for 19 and nine dimes and Miami stormed back to even the series, 115–78 in Game 2. The Heat would then close out the Bulls in five games as James led the way with 23 points, eight assists, and seven rebounds in the deciding contest before requiring a Game 7 to move past Paul George and the Indiana Pacers in the Eastern Conference Finals.

Despite a blistering attack from Frank Vogel's Indiana Pacers, led by 27 points from Paul George and 26 from David West, the Miami Heat hung on to win

LeBron holds the MVP trophy and the Larry O'Brien trophy after defeating the Spurs in the 2013 NBA Finals. (Steve Mitchell-USA TODAY Sports)

Game 1 of the 2013 Eastern Conference Finals. LeBron triple-doubled during the 103–102 victory, finishing with 30 points, 10 rebounds, and 10 assists. Wade added 19 while Bosh scored 17 and the Heat led the Pacers 1–0. But George would get 22 in Game 2 while Roy Hibbert emerged to score 29 points and collect 10 rebounds, and George Hill added 18 as Indiana evened the series with a four-point win. The Pacers would even the series again with a 14-point win in Game 6, to set up the Game 7 showdown on June 3, 2013, at American Airlines Arena in Miami, Florida, to decide the Conference Championship.

Miami's Big Three would spark a game-changing run during the second quarter that built a 15-point halftime lead for the Heat. James, Wade, Bosh, and company would win the third quarter of Game 7 by six points, and the fourth quarter by two, to establish the 23-point victory. LeBron had 32 points, eight rebounds, and four assists in Game 7 against the Pacers in the Eastern Conference Finals. Wade finished with 21 points and nine rebounds, while Bosh added a near double-double and Ray Allen scored 10 off the bench. The Heat were heading back to the NBA Finals for the third straight season, in search of their second straight NBA championship. They'd advance to find the Western Conference champion San Antonio Spurs, led once again by the great Tim Duncan, along with his Hall of Fame teammates, Tony Parker and Manu Ginobili. The Spurs also featured their next franchise player in All-NBA talent and Defensive Player of the Year Kawhi Leonard. The first four games would be split 2–2, as a pivotal Game 5 approached.

2013 NBA Finals

The Spurs starting five outscored the Heat starting five 107–73 on their way to securing the Game 5 victory and a 3–2 series lead in the 2013 NBA Finals. This was with LeBron James (25 points), Dwyane Wade (25 points), and Chris Bosh (16 points) scoring 66 points between them, while also accounting for 19 assists and 16 rebounds. Gregg Popovich's Spurs would use their true matchup advantage, All-Star caliber depth at the top of the lineup, going as deep as four players in Kawhi, and five on this night with 24 from Danny Green, in support of Timmy, Tony, and Manu. Game 6 would be historic, forever remembered as "The Ray Allen Game."

Kawhi had just converted 1-of-2 free throws to give the Spurs a 95–92 lead with 19.4 seconds remaining in Game 6 of the 2013 NBA Finals. The San Antonio Spurs were less than 20 seconds way from clinching another NBA championship. But with 6.3 seconds remaining in regulation, Chris Bosh would collect an offensive rebound resulting from a LeBron James three-point attempt, and kick the basketball out to the greatest pure shooter in NBA history who was at attention standing behind the three-point line. He received the pass from Bosh and released it as only Ray Allen does, 25-feet away from his target, and it found nothing but the bottom. The long-range bomb from Allen would tie the score at 95 with 5.2 seconds remaining in regulation. The Heat went on to win the game in overtime, 103–100. Miami won Game 7 of the 2013 NBA Finals 95–88, but it was Ray Allen saving them in Game 6 that would go down in history.

LeBron went for 37 points and 12 rebounds in Game 7 to win his second NBA championship ring. Wade added 23 points and 10 rebounds, while Shane Battier scored 18 off the bench to help secure the victory. LeBron averaged 25.3

points, 10.9 rebounds, and seven assists to earn NBA Finals MVP in 2013. It was the second straight season that LeBron had been named both the MVP of the NBA regular season, and the MVP of the NBA Finals. "This is what it's all about," James said following his second-straight championship with the Miami Heat. "I came here to win championships and to be able to go back to back, two championships in three years, so far, it's the ultimate."

Dwyane Wade averaged 20 points and four rebounds while bringing his third NBA championship to South Beach, and second straight alongside LeBron and Bosh. Despite struggling with injuries and his shot, the Heat's power forward member of the Big Three added 12 points and nine rebounds while Ray Allen scored 11 in the Finals.

Which brings me to this point in legacy building: Often, the greats in our game are advanced by the performance of their teammates, in big-time moments, which help determine the slimmest of margins. If Ray Allen, for example, doesn't hit that three off the Chris Bosh offensive rebound, that game will not be remembered for the Ray Allen miss, but the James miss that Bosh collected with six seconds left. But Jesus Shuttlesworth made history and LeBron added 10 Legacy Points after winning his fourth MVP (7 Legacy Points) and playing in another All-Star game (3 Legacy Points) to close the 2013 campaign with 75 Legacy Points.

Back-to-Back MVPs

LeBron James was the unanimous winner of the NBA's Most Valuable Player award during the 2012–13 season, in which he won his second championship. Behind the 28-year-old James, who would win the fourth MVP of his career, was a 24-year-old Kevin Durant, who finished second in the voting once again. New York Knicks All-Star forward Carmelo Anthony finished third, Los Angeles Clippers point guard Chris Paul finished fourth, and Los Angeles Lakers All-Star Kobe Bryant finished fifth. Teammate Dwyane Wade finished 10th in the 2013 MVP voting, while Tim Duncan and Kevin Garnett finished seventh and 12th.

The 2012 NBA Finals that LeBron's Heat won in five games against the Oklahoma City Thunder the season before would feature five players who finished in the top nine of the MVP voting the next season. While James and Wade finished first and 10th for Miami in 2013, Durant finished second, James Harden finished eighth and Russell Westbrook finished ninth when LeBron won his fourth MVP. These five players were all on the court together, along with perennial All-Star Bosh, comprising maybe the best pure collection of individual talent in recent NBA Finals history for one series. James, Wade, Bosh, Harden, Durant, and Westbrook—I would pay to see that game every single time they played it. And after winning that seismic battle of superstars, James and the Heat beat Tim Duncan, Tony Parker, Manu Ginobili, and Kawhi Leonard in seven games, thanks in part to an heroic heave by one of basketball's all-time great shooters in Ray Allen.

Chapter 23

★ ★ ★

Evolution of LeBron: Chris Bosh Effect

The causal NBA fans who essentially met Chris Bosh when he arrived in Miami never actually realized how good the Georgia Tech product truly was. As a top 10 pick in the same draft that gave us a kid from Akron named LeBron and a college baller from Marquette named Dwyane, Bosh's immediate impact was easily overshadowed. This was especially true when considering that Chris was the franchise player and annual All-Star for the only NBA basketball team who played their home games outside the United States. But by his second season as a professional, Bosh was established as a double-double machine for the Toronto Raptors. He played for roughly seven seasons in the NBA before being called soft or a wimp to some extent by basketball fans. This would occur in Miami while he was earning All-Star appearances and winning multiple NBA titles despite sacrificing personal numbers and allowing poorly educated sports fans to look at his scoring average and suggest he's not as good anymore.

As a teammate of LeBron's in Miami, Bosh would first learn what Kevin Love discovered later. He'd find out firsthand how difficult it is to fit in offensively with an aggressive mindset while playing alongside two ball-dominant superstars as a team's third leading scorer. For almost all of Bosh's professional career—and especially so first in Dallas as a high school superstar who attended ABCD camp with LeBron, to later an ACC standout at Georgia Tech—he was always his team's primary option. They won by how well he scored the ball. How well his teammates were able to space the floor for him. Screen for him specifically. Run plays designed to get Bosh the ball so he could score.

These dynamics changed so dramatically for Chris Bosh and later Kevin Love that the average basketball fan has a hard time comprehending what exactly it means to make sacrifices as an NBA player. But what it means is what Chris Bosh did: Accept a role as a team's third leading scorer, accentuate the areas of your game your teammates need you to be best at even if you are more comfortable playing a certain way, and opening yourself up for criticisms while attempting to make these sacrifices for your team. Without Chris Bosh doing all this at an elite level, LeBron does not win his first NBA championship ring. He would also not have won his second one, either.

Chris Bosh was able to pull opposing bigs out of the paint with his 15-foot jumper. He'd even eventually stretch that range out to three-point territory with solid consistency for a player his size. Bosh would hit big-time three-pointers in the postseason while securing two rings, and also post the double-doubles that earned him multiple All-Star appearances before arriving in South Beach. He rebounded and provided length around the basket, but what also made Bosh so special and important for LeBron was his leadership. Sometimes you need a teammate to smack you in the face and tell you that your actions are out of line and not helping the team if in fact that ever becomes the case. For one of the few times in their careers, Bosh was that voice for both Wade and James.

Bosh didn't have to agree to come join those guys and sacrifice his statistical accomplishments the way he did. He could get the max from any team in the NBA who had the cap space available. But he did, and if he saw his superstar teammates getting off track, he was the only player on the roster with the pedigree to check either of those two icons whenever necessary. This was one of the things that everyone knew about Chris Bosh, and one of the many reasons he was always truly respected by those who understood his brilliance.

Underrated Numbers

Chris Bosh averaged at least 22 points and eight rebounds for four straight seasons prior to joining LeBron on the Miami Heat in 2010. The Raptors All-Star

James hugs Bosh as they win the 2012 title. (AP Photo/Lynne Sladky)

center averaged 24 and 11 during his final season in Toronto. But as a member of the Big Three for the first time during the 2010–11 campaign, Bosh's numbers dipped to 18.7 points and 8.3 rebounds. The next three years in Miami, Bosh averaged 18 and 7.9, 16.6 and 6.8, and 16.2 and 6.6.

Before being sidelined with a scary and life-threatening blot clot along with several other competing issues related to this, Bosh averaged over 21 again as LeBron played out his first year in Cleveland. He essentially gave up roughly four to six points, or two to three field goals, per game to make the Big Three work the way it did in Miami.

Like Love, he was also forced to take more of his field goal attempts from the perimeter—as opposed to the paint—which moved him out of position for several rebounds. But when you look at the numbers on paper and remember the criticisms that seemed to circle Bosh at his every move on South Beach, it's odd to see how solid the numbers always were, as he improved his efficiencies at both ends of the floor.

It's also easy to see how Bosh helped LeBron win two more MVP awards as his teammate in Miami. Along with the two rings, LeBron would also play through the most efficient years of his career statistically as Bosh's teammate. He was certainly aided by the attention that Wade would receive on the opposite wing. But LeBron's ability to run pick-and-roll with Chris, and also find him around the rim while driving to the basket, are just some of the ways that Bosh helped LeBron play the most efficient basketball of his career. If it was just Wade and James, LeBron might have still put up the same overall numbers as far as total points, assists, and rebounds, but Bosh's versatility and spacing helped LeBron get those buckets more efficiently as he hung one John Hollinger ESPN PER title on top of another in Miami.

Bosh took bigs out of the paint and helped LeBron become the best version of himself as a player. Statistically, the metrics and two-man game scenarios could be found to support this claim. Even though all Bosh seemed to get was grief up until he helped silence the critics once and for all with the second title in 2013.

LeBron and Bosh Reunion Dream

I am typing this during the 2017 NBA All-Star Game. There is no evidence to support the claim that Chris Bosh will ever be medically cleared to return to the NBA. Athletically, he is obviously still capable of being an NBA starter for every team in the League in the very least. But according to doctors, the blood clot and related conditions (which I did not take enough schooling to truly understand) render him at risk to the rigors of NBA basketball. Prayers and modern medicine, however, help inspire basketball fans like me and others to whisper aloud how cool it might one day be to see Bosh come back for one more run alongside his former teammate, LeBron.

Maybe one year, Chris will be cleared and the medical consensus is that he can indeed return to play many more NBA seasons. That would be the real dream. But if that doesn't happen, maybe he has one or two more magical runs left in those CB4 high-tops. Maybe as we move past the trade deadline and collide towards the Playoffs one year, Bosh will become cleared and get picked up by LeBron James and his Cleveland Cavaliers. Or whatever team LeBron might be playing for in whatever year this hopefully one day happens. We need to see Bosh hit one more dagger. Make one more stop. Scowl one more time after blocking a critical shot. After collecting a pivotal rebound. After kicking it out for one more chance from distance. NBA basketball history is better for the fact that LeBron James and Chris Bosh learned to play alongside each other for a relatively short period of time, which resulted in four NBA Finals appearances and two rings. Our basketball future would be even better if we were blessed enough to see that again, if only for a series, game, half, or moment. Chris was and forever will be special.

Chapter 24

★ ★ ★

LeBron James vs. Magic Johnson

Earvin "Magic" Johnson
Professional Career: 1979–1991, 1996
NBA: Los Angeles Lakers
Legacy Points: 107 (No. 7)

Earvin "Magic" Johnson helped lead his team to an NBA championship as a 20-year-old rookie for the Los Angeles Lakers. He played his first professional game on October 12, 1979, against the San Diego Clippers, and earned a victory by scoring 26 points alongside a team-high 29 from Kareem Abdul-Jabbar. Six months later, Johnson was leading the Lakers onto the floor against a 55-win Phoenix Suns team for Game 1 of the Western Conference playoffs—a postseason stage he'd quickly take over.

Johnson would score 25 points in Game 2, while securing a three-point Lakers victory. Later, he'd close out the series with a 19-point effort as Los Angeles won by 25 in Game 5 to eliminate Phoenix. After losing Game 1 of the Western Conference Finals to the Seattle Supersonics 108–107, the Lakers would win the next four to eventually earn a matchup with Julius "Dr. J" Erving and the Philadelphia 76ers with the NBA title in the balance.

During Game 1 of Magic Johnson's first trip to the NBA Finals, his Lakers trailed the Philadelphia 76ers by two after one period. They'd tie things up at halftime, though, before exploding to a 31–17 advantage in the third quarter sparked by Johnson. The Lakers would win the game 109–102, despite 20 points from Dr. J. Kareem paced LA with 33, while a first-year floor general named Magic added 16.

With Erving, Daryl Dawkins, and Maurice Cheeks combining for 71 points, the Sixers won Game 2 to even the series. The Lakers would win three of the next four, however, and secure the NBA title in Johnson's first professional season. The rookie from Lansing, Michigan, averaged 18.3 points, 10.5 rebounds, 9.4 assists, and 3.1 steals during 16 playoff games in 1980. Along the way, he won his first of five NBA championships during a Hall of Famer career.

Magic's Lakers and Larry's Celtics

Magic helped the Los Angeles Lakers win the NBA title as a rookie in 1980. He'd also win in 1982, '85, '87, and '88. During those five championships, Magic's Lakers defeated the following teams led by the following legends:

- Philadelphia 76ers led by Julius Erving (1980)
- Philadelphia 76ers led by Julius Erving (1982)
- Boston Celtics led by Larry Bird (1985)
- Boston Celtics led by Larry Bird (1987)
- Detroit Pistons led by Isiah Thomas (1988)

The opponent that Magic is forever linked with, or the team he's most remembered competing against on basketball's biggest stage, was the Boston Celtics. From '84 to '88, the only two teams to win an NBA championship were Magic Johnson's Los Angeles Lakers and Larry Bird's Boston Celtics. The Celtics won in 1984 and '86. The Lakers won in 1985, '87, and '88. They'd match up against each other in the NBA Finals during three of those five seasons—'84, '85, and '87. Los Angeles vs. Boston. Lakers vs. Celtics. Magic vs. Bird. NBA basketball at its very best.

The Los Angeles Lakers traveled to Boston to collide with their Eastern Conference nemesis on May 27, 1984. After meeting to determine the NCAA national title in 1979, Magic and Bird were back on the championship stage as professionals. Rivals again, squaring off in Game 1 of the 1984 NBA Finals.

The Lakers point guard finished with 18 points, 10 assists, six rebounds, and four steals during that first NBA Finals matchup with the Celtics to help LA open the series with a 1–0 advantage. Meanwhile, Bird tossed in 24 to go along with grabbing 14 boards and dishing out five assists. With a game-high 32 from Kareem, the Lakers won 115–109.

Despite 27, 10, and nine from Magic in Game 2, the Celtics evened the series on the strength of a double-double from Bird. Johnson would go on to average 18 points, 14 assists, and eight rebounds during the seven-game series. In Game 4 he dished out 21 assists. Game 7, he finished with 16 points, 15 dimes, and five rebounds. Behind 20 and 12 from Bird, though, the Celtics would secure the 111–102 victory in Game 7 to win the NBA championship. Twelve months later, the two teams would meet again in the Finals for a rematch.

By the time the 1984–85 NBA regular season began, Magic was already wearing two championship rings. He had also won two NBA Finals MVP awards by that time, made four trips to the All-Star Game, and earned All-NBA status with his Hollywood flair and court vision. He led the League in assists and steals twice by then, as well, while earning lucrative endorsement deals off the court. Johnson had accomplished all this by the age of 25, as his sixth NBA season began on October 27, 1984, in San Antonio.

Led by legendary coach Pat Riley, the Lakers would lose on opening night of the regular season to the Spurs on the road. But by season's end, the Showtime Lakers won 62 games, after winning 54 a year earlier. Los Angeles would open the playoffs by winning their first six games, too—sweeping the Phoenix Suns, and getting out to a 3–0 advantage against the Portland Trailblazers. They'd then eliminate Portland in Game 5, and use the same number of games to advance past the Denver Nuggets in the Western Conference Finals.

The Celtics and Lakers were set to tip off again in the NBA Finals on May 27, 1985.

Magic would make his fifth trip to the NBA All-Star game in 1985. He averaged 18.3 points, 12.6, assists and 6.2 rebounds per game in 77 appearances during the regular season. He shot 56 percent from the floor and 84 percent from the free-throw line. It was the only season—one in which he averaged over *12 dimes per night*—that Magic did not lead the NBA in assists during a five-year span from 1983–87. He was the best playmaker in basketball—a 6'9" basketball god who could whip passes from anywhere.

Behind a balanced attack from the defending NBA champions, the Boston Celtics made a statement in Game 1 of the 1985 Finals. Despite 19 points and 12 assists from Magic, the Lakers were blown out 148–114. But Los Angeles would hit back in Game 2. The Lakers built a 31–26 lead over the Celtics in the first quarter, before managing a seven-point victory, 109–102. Magic would help lead a 25-point victory in Game 3, as well, before winning the NBA championship in six games over the team who beat him last year. Revenge was spelled with Magic, as the Los Angeles hero averaged 18, 14, and seven throughout the Finals. He was an NBA champion three times over well before his 30th birthday.

Magic and Kareem

Earvin "Magic" Johnson and Kareem Abdul-Jabbar were teammates with the Los Angeles Lakers for 10 seasons. From the moment Johnson was drafted in 1979, until the season Kareem retired, Magic and Kareem were the most devastating one-two punch in all of basketball. An innovative point guard, a dominating center, they formed arguably the most underrated all-time great duo in the history of professional basketball. They were Showtime. They were the best.

During the 10 seasons that Kareem and Magic played together in LA, they went to the NBA Finals eight times. They won five NBA championships during this stretch, losing three, while also getting as far as the Western Conference Finals, advancing to the playoffs every season they played together. Statistically, the raw numbers are staggering. From 1980 to '89, Magic and Kareem combined to average the following:

Points: 40.1

Rebounds: 14

Assists: 15

Kareem won MVPs before Magic. Johnson won MVPs after Jabbar. Individually, they are two of the greatest players to ever live. From an offensive perspective—while Magic led the NBA in steals twice during this stretch, and Kareem led once in blocks—they accounted for roughly 70 points per night of offense when considering the points and assists they averaged as a tandem. They were simply unstoppable.

Cultural Icon

Earvin Johnson was everything you hope a professional athlete could be. He was an innovative player who approached the game with unbridled joy. He was dedicated to making those around him better. He was a point guard. He was a leader. He was a fierce competitor. Famous rival. He was also a great team-mate with a nickname that captured his very essence. He was charismatic, an engaging spokesman. He was special, he was magical in the way he moved the basketball.

Johnson may have played through the mid-1990s had he not been infected with the HIV virus, which led to his abrupt retirement in 1991. He sat out the next four seasons before returning at age 36 to play 32 more games with LA, then finally hanging up his legendary sneakers for good in 1996. He'd teach us all through his work to raise awareness for HIV and AIDS in his life after basketball to always believe. To always hope. It was never over. He'd teach us how to dream, and we'd watch him apply those dreams to businesses he'd eventually build into an empire.

The proud Michigan State alum would open several movie theaters as a successful business mogul continuing to inspire those in the African American community to reach for greatness on and off the basketball court. He'd open several Starbucks coffee shops, too, and he'd make enough money to buy the Los Angeles Dodgers. Throughout his entire life, he'd continue to assist. He'd continue to post numbers. He was an entertainer who owns five NBA championships and three MVP awards.

In February 2017, Magic Johnson was hired as an advisor to Los Angeles Lakers owner Jeanie Buss. Johnson was tasked with restructuring the basketball operations for a franchise that has struggled since the passing of Jeanie's father, the legendary Jerry Buss, who helped guide LA to double-digit NBA championships. If Magic's track record means anything, there's a good chance his old team will be winning again in the next few years.

LeBron vs. Magic Johnson

Legacy Power Rankings: 97 vs. 107
Johnson:
- **MVP award: 3 (21)**
- **NBA championship: 5 (50)**
- **NBA All-Star: 12 (36)**

LEBRON JAMES VS. THE NBA

Magic has five NBA championship rings compared to three for LeBron heading into the 2017 NBA Finals. He also played in the same number of All-Star Games as James at this point in his career. LeBron has one more MVP. For those reasons, Magic currently occupies the No. 6 spot on the Basketball Legacy Power Rankings list with 13 more points than James.

From a young age, it was always easy to agree that LeBron was more Magic than Michael. They were both big guards who were savants with the basketball. This unselfishness combined with creativity, skill, athleticism, vision, and determination will forever link Magic and LeBron together. To earn more Legacy Points than Johnson, LeBron would need to add at least one championship and two All-Star game appearances (16 points). One MVP award and one championship (17 points) following his third in 2016 would also move James past Magic on this list. We are predicting that James will account for some combination of those totals to move past Earvin before he retires from basketball.

Chapter 25

★ ★ ★

LeBron James vs. Tim Duncan

Tim Duncan
Professional Career: 1997–2016
NBA: San Antonio Spurs
Legacy Points: 109 (No. 6)

Tim Duncan built his Hall of Fame career by climbing the fundamental basketball ladder to the very top. Even though he never said much, or caught our attention off the court too often, it happened. He dominated for two decades. Duncan was a simple player. The game, the world, it was simple for him. It was fair. Put in work and you give yourself a chance to succeed. He lived as he played, by his principles. Attack with this, he'll give you that. Drop step, or, from 15 with that sweet sound off the board only Bill Raftery can describe. Duncan just beat you. He was fundamentally brilliant—Mikan Drill extraordinaire.

Duncan was a leader not just for his team, or his franchise, but also his fellow players around the League throughout his career. Sensitive to the work stoppages NBA labor disputes could create—after experiencing the 1999 lockout as a second-year player—Duncan didn't hesitate to speak when the moment required. He was a college graduate from Wake Forest University who dominated the hardwood stateside ever since arriving from Saint Croix (US Virgin Islands). And his opinion mattered.

"I think it's a load of crap," Tim Duncan was quoted as saying to the *San Antonio Express-News* on October 19, 2005, after the NBA dress code was announced. "I understand what they're trying to do with [forbidding] hats and 'do rags and [retro] jerseys and stuff. That's fine. But I don't understand why they would take it to this level."

Duncan spoke out at the time as a 28-year-old veteran of the League who had just won the NBA championship in June of that year. The title would be the third that Duncan would help the San Antonio Spurs secure since arriving in 1997. He was an eight-time All-NBA First Team selection at this point. He didn't dress cool. But he didn't dress like Dipset too often, either, though he publicly respected his colleagues' right to do so if they chose.

"I don't like the direction they're going," the former No.1 overall draft pick added in response to the ruling. "But who am I?"

Duncan's quotes cleared the lane for others around the League to offer their honest opinions as well in response to the new Dress Code Policy. Future teammate Stephen Jackson—then with the Indiana Pacers—were among those who questioned the dress code.

"I have no problem dressing up," Pacers guard Stephen Jackson admitted to the Indianapolis Star. "Because I know I'm a nice-looking guy. But as far as chains, I definitely feel that's a racial statement. Almost 100 percent of the guys in the league who are young and black wear big chains. So I definitely don't agree with that at all."

Meanwhile, the coach of the team that Duncan's San Antonio Spurs would battle for many championships throughout their years in the Western Conference weighed in on the new NBA dress code as well.

"The players have been dressing in prison garb the last five or six years," Los Angeles Lakers Coach Phil Jackson is quoted as saying to the *San Gabriel Valley Tribune* on October 19. "All the stuff that goes on, it's like gangster, thuggery stuff. It's time. It's been time to do that. But one must remember where one came from. I was wearing bib overalls when I was a player one time. But I wasn't going to the games or events in them."

An Admiral Introduction

Tim Duncan's lifelong legend would crash shores of friendly beaches when it landed in NBA waters patrolled by David Robinson. In 1998, the Naval hero nicknamed the Admiral—one of the NBA's 50 Greatest Players—was back to his dominant self after being injured the year before, as Timmy was wrapping up his senior year in college. Robinson was a willing teacher, Duncan a student of the game, and they played the way a young coach named Gregg Popovich asked them to play. The Twin Towers had officially arrived in San Antonio.

Duncan appeared in all 82 games during his first professional season, averaging 21.1 points and 11.9 rebounds and winning NBA Rookie of the Year honors in 1998. Meanwhile, Robinson offered 21.6 and 10.6 alongside his talented young teammate. The towering duo would combine to average 37.5 points and 21.4 rebounds the following year, while eliminating points in the paint for seemingly all opponents with their suffocating defense at the rim.

On June 16, 1999, that journey would collide with Jeff Van Gundy's New York Knicks for Duncan's first shot at basketball immortality. Led by a freewheeling Knicks team who was forced to quickly find a new identity of sorts after losing Patrick Ewing to injury before Game 3 of the Eastern Conference Finals, Latrell Spreewell and Allan Houston emerged to carry the scoring load for New York as the series began. While attempting to pepper the two Spurs giants with a combination of pinpoint jump shots, timely drives, and transition points, the two Knicks tossed in 19 each. New York—who qualified for the playoffs as the No. 8 seed before beating Miami, Atlanta, and Indiana to advance to the Finals—was leading 27–21 as the first quarter concluded.

But Duncan's dominance would make its first Finals appearance. Timmy finished with 33 points and 16 rebounds in Game 1. Robinson added a near triple-double with 13 points, nine rebounds, and seven assists. Meanwhile, future NBA coaches Avery Johnson and Steve Kerr combined for six points and eight assists for San Antonio.

The Spurs went on to defeat the scrappy Knicks in five games. Duncan averaged 27.4 points and 14 rebounds. He was named NBA Finals MVP for the first of what would be three times in his career for his debut performance on basketball's biggest stage. Four seasons later, Duncan, Pop, and the Spurs would win their second title together, and first of three that were captured every other year from 2003 to '07.

Tim would add one more alongside longtime teammates Tony Parker and Manu Ginobili in 2014 to retire with five rings. But his Hall of Fame ticket was punched long before then.

Back-to-Back MVPs

Two straight seasons recognized as the best player in basketball, or the NBA MVP, is difficult to accomplish. The list of players who did it before Duncan achieved the feat in 2002 and '03 includes the following: Bill Russell, Wilt Chamberlain, Kareem Abdul-Jabbar, Moses Malone, Larry Bird, Magic Johnson, and Michael Jordan.

The numbers that Duncan hung on NBA scoreboards throughout this two-year MVP run were simply astounding. He averaged 24.4 points and 12.8 rebounds while appearing in 163 regular season games. The Spurs won 118 of those games (58 and 60) while winning the '03 championship. The year before, in 2002, San Antonio advanced to the Western Conference Semifinals before falling to Shaq and Kobe's Lakers in five games. This was despite a career-best postseason scoring average of 27.6 points from Duncan during the playoffs.

It is at precisely this moment—following the 2003 NBA Finals—that Duncan had actually done enough to make a claim to be the greatest power forward of all-time based on his skill, talent, and production. But it wasn't until years later that he was universally accepted as such.

Heading into the 2003–04 campaign, the former swimming champion from the Virgin Islands who college coaching legend Dave Odom recruited to join his team at Wake Forest had already accomplished the following in the NBA:

- 2x NBA Champion
- 2x NBA Finals MVP
- 2x NBA regular season MVP
- 5x NBA All-Star
- 6x First Team All-NBA Player

This was Tim Duncan at age 26, five years into his professional career. San Antonio would win three more titles from there with Timmy—and maybe could've even won more?

Perennial Winning

Tim Duncan lost in the NBA Finals only once. In 2013, LeBron James, Dwyane Wade, Chris Bosh, and the Miami Heat got the better of San Antonio with help from an all-time great shot by Ray Allen. In addition to advancing to six NBA Finals (winning five), Duncan also proved his evergreen skill set could succeed in any area of NBA basketball. He won his first title in 1999, and his final title 15 years later in 2014. Much had changed over that decade and a half, but Duncan remained a constant force.

His seasons also ended in the Western Conference Finals three more times. This makes nine seasons of advancing at least as far as the Conference Finals for Duncan, with more than half of those trips ending in rings. He was an NBA All-Defensive Team player 15 times in his career and selected to 15 All-Star Games. He helped his teammates develop, his coaches grow. He was more than a franchise pillar. He was the foundation, walls, and rafters of the best organization in the NBA. He was special in his simplicity that way.

Duncan's final season in 2016 included a 67-win regular season—one of the best all-time—and concluded with a Western Conference Semifinals defeat at the hands of Kevin Durant, Russell Westbrook, and the Oklahoma City Thunder in six games.

Duncan was a legend who inspired the greatest to ever play the game. LeBron James was among the many NBA players to congratulate Duncan on Twitter upon retirement.

"Timmy D you know how I feel about you, what you did for me and for the entire NBA," James tweeted. "Thank you for an amazing career! #BestPFEver #Legend"

Duncan didn't hold a press conference during the summer of 2016 to announce his retirement from basketball. He didn't issue a statement on social media or write an article in *The Players Tribune*. He told his boss and his teammates, and he left. There was nothing more to say. He was done. The best power forward of all-time and one of professional sports' greatest leaders. That was Tim Duncan—The Big Fundamental.

LeBron vs. Tim Duncan

Legacy Power Rankings: 97 vs. 109

Duncan:

- **MVP award: 2 (14)**
- **NBA championship: 5 (50)**
- **NBA All-Star: 15 (45)**

Tim Duncan is often overlooked when discussing the very best basketball players to ever live. But the Legacy Power Rankings List—that factors a combination of championship rings, MVP awards, and All-Star appearances—slots Duncan near the very top. He retired from the NBA just two Legacy Points behind Kobe Bryant (111), while only Jordan, Abdul-Jabbar, and Russell totaled more than the great Spurs big man in League history.

Entering the 2016–17 NBA playoffs, LeBron James trailed Duncan by 12 Legacy Points with 97. One MVP award and one NBA championship, following LeBron's first in Cleveland, would be enough to move past Duncan on the Legacy Power Rankings. Either one of those two accomplishments, combined with five more All-Star appearances, would also be enough.

Chapter 26

★ ★ ★

Final Season in South Beach

LeBron James concluded his fourth season in Miami as a 10-time All-Star, four-time MVP, and two-time NBA champion. He would play his last game alongside Dwyane Wade and Chris Bosh for the Miami Heat on June 15, 2014. By that point, he'd earned 78 Legacy Points and remained in what would be No. 13 position all-time behind Larry Bird and Wilt Chamberlain with 87 Legacy Points. By winning two championships, two MVPs and appearing in four more All-Star Games, LeBron earned 46 Legacy Points in Miami. That was good for 14 more than he earned during his first seven years with the Cleveland Cavaliers.

In LeBron's final game for Micky Arison, Pat Riley, Erik Spoelstra, and the Miami Heat, he scored 31 points and collected 10 rebounds while also dishing out five assists in 41 minutes. Bosh added 13 and seven, Wade scored 11 and no other member of the Heat reached double figures as the San Antonio Spurs secured Tim Duncan's fifth and final championship in 2014.

During the regular season, LeBron scored 30 or more points 31 different times. He also added one triple-double and 11 double-doubles to his NBA resume as Miami compiled a 54–28 record. James, Wade, Bosh, and the Heat would then use nine games to move past the Charlotte Bobcats and Brooklyn Nets to match up once again with their longtime Eastern Conference nemesis, Paul George and the Indiana Pacers.

The Miami Heat needed only six games to eliminate the well-coached and highly competitive group of Pacers led by George (24.2 series ppg), David West (16.2 series ppg), and Lance Stephenson (14 series ppg). James would use 22.8 points, 6.3 rebounds, and 5.5 assists to qualify for his fourth straight NBA Finals and fifth overall appearance of his NBA career. Wade averaged 19.8 and Bosh averaged 16.2 to send the South Beach trio back to the Finals against Gregg Popovich's San Antonio Spurs. This would be the second straight season the Heat would meet the Spurs in the NBA Finals, and third time for LeBron overall in his career, dating back to the 2007 Cavs-Spurs Finals.

Record-Setting Streak of NBA Finals Appearances

LeBron James appeared in four-straight NBA Finals for the Miami Heat from 2011–14. He had been to the NBA Finals five times before his 30th birthday. Michael Jordan made his fifth trip to the NBA Finals in 1997, as a 33-year-old shooting guard for the Chicago Bulls. The Nike pitchman and Babe Ruth of basketball's modern era who was six-for-six in NBA Finals appearances would win this third championship at 29 years old—the same age LeBron was during his final season with Miami. But it would take LeBron two more seasons after that to eventually secure ring No. 3 in what had once seemed the most unlikely of places.

By the time James did secure ring No. 3 of his NBA career, he did so by delivering the Cleveland Cavaliers its first championship in franchise history in 2016. He was 31. Air Jordan won his fourth title for the Bulls when he returned after a hiatus in baseball in 1996. When he closed out the series and celebrated ring No. 4 with cigars and Scottie Pippen in the Chicago locker room, the great Michael Jordan was 33 years and 120 days old. LeBron turns 33 on December 30, 2018, and can keep pace with Jordan by coming back from the 2017 Finals loss with another ring.

The fact that Jordan never lost a series on the NBA's biggest stage is remarkable. It adds to his invincibility and rule over the basketball kingdom during his time on top of the game. But that shouldn't lessen the fact that LeBron has now gone to seven straight NBA Finals and won eight conference championships throughout his career. He's won at least three with two different teams (Cleveland and Miami) and consistently competes for a ring every season. Does he need to win at least five or six championships to truly enter the GOAT conversation with Jordan? Yes. But once he accomplishes that, to also feature this string of conference dominance along with five or six rings and four or five MVPs will be more of a feather in LeBron's all-time great argument than many of us imagined as we watched him lose in the NBA Finals.

To put LeBron's NBA Finals appearance totals (eight NBA Finals appearances through 2017) in perspective, Bill Russell appeared in 12 NBA Finals. Magic Johnson appeared in nine NBA Finals, Kobe seven, Jordan six, Tim Duncan six. LeBron has more than any other historically great player after that. He lost one time with the Cavs when he shouldn't have even qualified for the Finals in 2007, twice with Miami (in their first and last seasons together), and once back in Cleveland during his first year with Kyrie Irving and Kevin Love. The 2014 title was one James should've probably claimed. In 2014, the Miami Heat were going for a three-peat, most recently accomplished by Shaq and Kobe's Lakers and Michael and Scottie's Bulls. But the Heat would split trips to the NBA Finals during LeBron's four seasons in Miami, and fall to Timmy D and his Spurs in five games in 2014.

The Miami Heat dynasty was blown to pieces for all eternity during the 2014 NBA Finals. LeBron was the NBA MVP during the regular season and the NBA Finals for two straight years heading into his final national tour alongside a group that some nicknamed the Heatles. But one two-point victory would be it for LeBron and the Heat in their final appearance in the NBA Finals. The Spurs would win big in the final three games, and eventually send Pat Riley's franchise back to the drawing board after four years of basketball brilliance.

Bosh, Wade, and the Summer of '14

When the highly decorated Big Three first teamed up in 2010, they were three perennial All-Stars each in the prime of their respective careers, all still yet to celebrate their 30th birthday. But by the summer of 2014, following LeBron's fourth season in Miami, both James and Bosh would celebrate their 29th birthdays, while the elder statesman, Wade, turned 32.

The 2013–14 season would also tragically be the last season that Bosh may ever play throughout an entire regular season and playoffs of his Hall of Fame career. First with injuries, and later an extremely serious medical condition that kept him from the court, Bosh would go on to appear in only 97 regular season games over the next two years before starting the 2016–17 campaign as not part of an active roster.

Wade, meanwhile, who was a top five player in the League when James and Bosh first arrived, was beginning to show his age and professional mileage. Specifically, the toll from those punches from bigger defenders from early in his career, when the young Marquette product regularly finished at the rim with reckless abandon. Wade scored 19 points per night when he was playing, but only appeared in 54 games during the last regular season he'd spend as LeBron's teammate in Miami. He'd play 62 and 74 games for the Heat over the next two seasons after that, before signing with the Chicago Bulls in 2016. Throughout that post-LeBron stretch, Wade averaged just over 19 points and almost five assists to go along with four rebounds through 2017.

After spending four seasons in Miami, James would shock the professional sports landscape by announcing his return to The Land in the pages of *Sports Illustrated* as presented to us by James and the great Lee Jenkins. LeBron would be reuniting with his hometown Cleveland Cavaliers and accept the challenge of delivering the city its first professional sports championship in over 50 years. He wouldn't win the five, or six, or seven championships he boasted about prematurely upon arrival in Miami, but LeBron did lead his team to multiple championships with the Heat. He'd also win the Eastern Conference four times, and secure two more MVP awards before The Return to Northeast Ohio for LeBron to start the 2014–15 season.

A Teammate Named Champ

To know James Jones is to respectfully refer to him by the name he worked hard to earn among NBA circles: "Champ." Jones was selected No. 49 overall by the Indiana Pacers in the same 2003 draft in which the Cavs took LeBron No. 1. In two seasons with Indiana, Jones appeared in 81 games and averaged 4.7 points per contest. He shot 39.4 percent from three-point range as a 6'8" forward who would work on the defensive end and slowly began to catch the attention of teams around the League as a winning player.

Over the next two seasons, Jones would earn 20.8 minutes per night off the Phoenix Suns bench as a spot starter who averaged eight points and three rebounds. After 58 more games for Portland, Champ signed with the Miami Heat in the summer of 2008. During his third season with the Heat in 2010–11, Jones became teammates with LeBron James for the first time. They would make seven straight NBA Finals appearances during the first seven years they spent together as teammates.

In 2011, '12, '13, and '14, Jones, James, and the Miami Heat appeared in the NBA Finals. Champ would then go in support of James' mission to deliver Northeast Ohio its first NBA title, and appear in the 2015, 2016, and 2017 NBA Finals as a Cleveland Cavalier. He is precisely the type of player that championship teams are built with, and one who LeBron has called his favorite teammate of all-time.

Heading into the 2017 NBA Finals, the 36-year-old sharpshooter from Miami, Florida, has appeared in just over 700 regular season games. During that time, over the last dozen years, Jones has averaged 5.2 points and 1.8 rebounds. His career high was 9.3 points for the season in 24 minutes per game with the Suns in 2006. But what James Jones also was, and is, cannot be quantified. He is the teammate who tells the best player to keep shooting just before he makes that critical shot. He can offer advice like a golf coach when you're missing your three, and spread the floor offensively by knocking down over 40 percent of his triples as a pro. That's why they call him Champ. He was a player and person you win with both on and off the court, just like LeBron did in Miami and Cleveland.

Chapter 27

★ ★ ★

The Return

LeBron James announced his intentions to sign with his hometown Cavaliers and return to Cleveland through the pages of *Sports Illustrated* on July 12, 2014. In a message that the great Lee Jenkins helped James finalize, LeBron highlighted his goal of delivering a championship to Northeast Ohio. The two-time NBA champion and four-time MVP would accept his legacy being recapped, in part, and aligned with his ability to secure at least one more ring and the first in franchise history for the team who drafted him. But LeBron's decision would mean much more than dunks and championships, especially for the children in the same Northeast Ohio housing projects from which James emerged.

"I want kids in Northeast Ohio, like the hundreds of Akron third-graders I sponsor through my foundation, to realize that there's no better place to grow up," James wrote in *Sports Illustrated*. "Maybe some of them will come home after college and start a family or open a business. That would make me smile. Our community, which has struggled so much, needs all the talent it can get. In Northeast Ohio, nothing is given. Everything is earned. You work for what you have. I'm ready to accept the challenge. I'm coming home."

"LeBron to these kids is like Michael Jordan for us," coach Chet Mason said in an article published at StepienRules.com the morning after LeBron announced his return to the Cavaliers. Mason was running a free inner-city basketball camp at Zelma George Recreation Center in Cleveland that I attended and wrote about on my Cavs blog. The site of Mason's free camp to exercise and learn basketball fundamentals from professional players was not far from where Tamir Rice was trag-ically taken. "LeBron is everything for these kids. If they don't know anything, they know who LeBron James is. So they're excited, and it's electric in here right now."

Over 200 students of all ages poured through the Cleveland recreation center's doors for Mason's eighth annual free basketball camp for students the day after LeBron announced his return to Cleveland. Coach Mason played professional basketball for a dozen years before recently retiring. He was named Most Valuable Player of the Adriatic League in 2010, and returned home each summer to organize a series of vol-unteer efforts designed to inspire and support the urban youth from his hometown.

"With LeBron, it's not just about the basketball," Mason explained. "He's so powerful. He inspires these kids and he also impacts the economy so significantly. There wasn't as much money being generated around here when he left. While he was with the Cavs, people were flying in from Vegas and California and Chicago, bringing the money they spent with them to Northeast Ohio. When that was hap-pening, you're creating more jobs for our inner-city kids. The businesses around the arena are hiring more people. The Q is going to be hiring more people. The wing spots, the restaurants, they're all going to be giving these inner-city kids jobs again now that he's back. It's amazing to think about the overall impact he'll have on so many levels."

Mason's relationship with James dates back to junior high school. In 2000, Chet "The Jet" Mason was named Mr. Basketball in the state of Ohio as a senior guard from Cleveland South. The following season, a sophomore from St. Vincent-St. Mary in Akron named LeBron James won his first of three Mr. Basketball Awards in Ohio. Mason played for the legendary Charlie Coles at Miami University for four seasons after starring in Cleveland's Senate League. He was not selected in the NBA draft but went on to spend a preseason in 2007 as LeBron's teammate on the Cavs preliminary roster. Mason also appeared for the Lakers in the preseason as well as a number of D-League stops and overseas contracts.

"I've known LeBron since he was in sixth grade," Mason said. "They'd be coming up to Cleveland to play and I've known him on a personal level ever since. He's always been a great guy and I can't tell you how much it means to this area for him to come home. You can feel it in this gym. You can see it with these kids and you can see it on the street. He means so much. The kids in this community, they understand that and they're excited to have him back."

LeBron walks into the stadium with his family after being introduced for his homecoming on August 8, 2014, in Akron, Ohio. (AP Photo/Tony Dejak)

Back to the NBA Finals

The Cavaliers would ride the momentum of a midseason trade during LeBron's 2014–15 season back in Cleveland and eventually hit their stride in time to win the Eastern Conference title. They'd advance to the NBA Finals for a matchup with the Western Conference champion Golden State Warriors led by Stephen Curry and Klay Thompson. In a series of moves, the Cavs traded away Dion Waiters and Anderson Varejao along with other pieces in order to satisfy NBA trade agreements. In return, they netted Iman Shumpert, J.R. Smith, and Timofey Mozgov.

Smith and Shumpert added much needed backcourt depth while Mozgoz provided some help up front. The underrated big man proved to be a critical piece of the conference-champion Cavs, and had experience playing for Cavs head coach David Blatt as a member of the Russian National Team. It seemed like a good fit at the time, and helped make a positive impact very quickly in anchoring the Cavaliers around the basket. If the team was not besieged by critical injuries from there, who knows? But the Warriors proved to be deserving champions and emerged from a 2–1 deficit to win the series on the road in six as the Cavaliers fought valiantly without the services of Kyrie Irving and Kevin Love.

Irving made the All-Star team during his first season with LeBron. Love worked the hardest individually to make the Big Three a cohesive force, and his numbers suffered because of it. He did not make the All-Star team, and some people didn't appreciate his versatility and the changes he was making to his game, but he was still very good. So no Irving and no Love and the Cavaliers had LeBron and a Matthew Dellavedova possessed with passion, but it still wasn't enough to get it done. Without Kyrie or Kevin the Cavaliers won Game 3 of the NBA Finals to take a 2–1 lead. But without Kyrie and Kevin they wouldn't win again from there.

If ever a representative of the losing team deserved to win the NBA Finals MVP award, it was LeBron James during the 2015 NBA Finals. The last and only other time a losing player was ever named NBA Finals MVP was when Jerry West accomplished the feat in 1969 for the Los Angeles Lakers. If LeBron didn't do enough in 2015 to re-claim that honor, then it will never happen again. In 100 years, it will still be the Logo as the last person to ever be named MVP of a team that lost the NBA Finals. But LeBron certainly deserved to be in that conversation.

In Games 1–6, LeBron scored: 44, 39, 40, 20, 40, and 32 points; collected eight, 16, 12, 12, 14, and 18 rebounds; along with six, 11, eight, eight, 11, and nine assists. He was undoubtedly the best individual in the series and also posted a 39-point, 16-rebound, 11-assist triple-double in Game 2, as well as a 40, 14, and 11 triple-double in Game 5. He had two triple-doubles *in the series*. LeBron James scored at least 39 in four games and averaged 13 rebounds in the NBA Finals.

Andre Igoudala won the MVP award for being the most consistent Golden State Warriors player and he certainly impacted in all phases of the game. But LeBron was the most valuable, even in defeat, and it wasn't close.

LeBron James Factor

The Cavaliers averaged just over 17,000 fans per night during LeBron's final season with the Miami Heat. During the 2014–15 campaign, the Cavaliers averaged 20,562. The Cavaliers also won 53 games under David Blatt on their way to the 2015 NBA Finals after winning only 33 and missing the playoffs the year before James arrived. The Cavs would add Kevin Love in 2014, too, but Love was never agreeing to a trade to a LeBron-less Cleveland team. LeBron single-handedly transformed the franchise from the perennial loser it was before he arrived in 2003 and the perennial loser it became again for the four years he was gone. The Cavs were a title contender based solely on the fact that LeBron agreed to play for them. It takes a special player to make that much of an impact as one individual, but that's the type of player that LeBron has always been.

Legacy Power Rankings

James would make another sharp leap up the Legacy Points Power Rankings during his second season with the Cavaliers but he wouldn't quite pass anyone during Year 1. Still directly ahead of Moses Malone and just behind Bird and Chamberlain, LeBron would need to win his third championship the following year to have a legitimate chance of chasing the ghost of Michael Jordan and the 137 Legacy Points he racked up before retiring and buying an NBA franchise.

Even though it appeared that James was on the brink of a championship run in Cleveland alongside a young and emerging Kyrie Irving and Kevin Love, all was not well in the Cavaliers kingdom. As he had with Mike Brown and Erik Spoelstra before, James had come under scrutiny for several public exchanges with coach David Blatt. He'd also famously say on the way to the NBA Finals that he changed a play that Blatt diagramed during the Chicago series to a play where he hit the game winner. This public shaming of sorts and general appearance of a disconnect would not go away despite the wins in year one. If Love and Irving had been healthy enough, maybe LeBron and Blatt win and play on for many seasons together. But they weren't healthy in 2015, and it began to seem more and more likely that would be the only chance that Blatt would get at winning big in Cleveland.

Chapter 28

★ ★ ★

Evolution of LeBron: Kyrie Irving Effect

James was a reigning NBA champion and MVP when he cheered on Eastern Conference All-Star teammate Kyrie Irving during the 2013 NBA Three-Point Shootout. As the young and emerging superstar point guard from the Cleveland Cavaliers buried triple after triple to win the All-Star Weekend event, James continued to show his support as the TNT cameras caught him on the sideline of the fan-friendly event. James would go on to find Irving—and vice versa—during the All-Star game that Sunday, previewing what would eventually become one of the NBA's deadliest one-two punches.

James was tough on Irving early on in their tenure together. As a veteran who won MVPs and titles, he quickly learned that Kyrie was an elite talent. LeBron took it upon himself to help develop Irving and the results would show up in spades during the 2016 NBA Finals.

As LeBron James put together the three best postseason games of his career in back-to-back-to-back fashion to not only force a Game 7 but also win it, Irving was getting huge buckets in support of the King. He'd go for well over 30 in each of the pivotal games before hitting the long range bomb heard around the world as he sealed Cleveland's championship victory with the go-ahead triple. But it was long before that NBA Finals series that Irving began to prove his worth as an

MVP caliber player. After suffering a series of injuries during the 2015 playoffs, before going out entirely in Game 1 of the Finals, Irving came roaring back from injury upon his debut the following season. Playing on the road in a non-descript game against the Wizards, Irving began his charge in earnest for the greatness that LeBron declared his point guard teammate to possess.

Return from Injury in Pursuit of Rings

Kyrie Irving pulled up in the nation's capital five feet beyond the arc with 1:45 remaining in a January 6 matchup with Washington Wizards. He let loose on a long-range jumper that climbed over the outstretched hand of a defender before slicing through the net to give his Cleveland Cavaliers a 119–105 lead that they'd never relinquish. He'd hit a similar triple over an outstretched hand of Curry later in the Finals, but this effort would come against All-Star John Wall. The three-point field goal capped off a 32-point effort from Irving in the wake of six-plus months of bone-rattling rehab. After missing the first 24 games of the 2015–16 season due to a broken kneecap suffered in Game 1 of the NBA Finals—and two of the previous eight heading into Washington—the godson of Rod Strickland proved he was still very much capable of making defenders jump. He would also demonstrate shortly after that night that he was only getting started from there.

"Coming into that fourth quarter, I just wanted to be aggressive, not only for myself but for my teammates," Irving said after the game. "They were hitting some tough shots, they got it going, cut down our lead. LeBron gets it going in the third quarter, he gets a bunch of threes and the game is still close. They continued to battle. I mean, their transition game is unbelievable, led by John Wall. They're getting it going no matter what, got some transition threes but we got timely stops in the fourth quarter."

That postgame comment essentially summarized the player that LeBron encouraged Kyrie to become upon his arrival in Cleveland. As a Rookie of the Year and All-Star before James arrived, it was evident that Kyrie could ball. But James knew what was required to be great and he'd push Irving during their time together to be even more aggressive. He'd help him understand that Kyrie was not being selfish by attacking the basket or knocking down a triple. He was spreading the floor. He was loosening up the defense. He was creating shots for others. This effort, meshed with LeBron's greatness, would eventually lead, for Irving, from that grueling injury rehab to the NBA Finals podium in less than 12 months. But it would never be easy for LeBron, Kyrie, or any of their teammates along the way.

Rookie Sensation Back in Cleveland

LeBron James won the NBA's Rookie of the Year Award in 2003. Kyrie Irving won the award in 2012. No Cavaliers player would win that award in the meantime and nobody else has ever won it since. Despite a series of untimely injuries, however, the No. 1 overall pick of the 2011 NBA Draft had proven to be one of the most unique talents in basketball by his fourth season in the League. He combined one of the best crossovers since Allen Iverson with a world-class jump shot to earn Rookie of the Year honors and multiple trips to the All-Star game. At 6'3", the 25-year-old point guard's ability to also play the off-guard position blended well with LeBron James, helping to form one of the most dynamic one-two punches in the Association. During their first season as teammates, Irving averaged 21.7 points and 5.2 assists. LeBron, meanwhile, averaged 25.3 points, 7.4, assists, and six rebounds. Together, they'd close out the 2014–15 campaign accounting for 70-plus points per night when considering combined points and assists (47 points, 12.6 assists). Kyrie averaged 20 points and five assists the following year while LeBron posted 25 points and seven dimes. The more time they spent together as teammates the more deadly they continue to become for opposing defenses. You can load up to stop James and you can load up to stop Irving on defense, but you can't load up to stop both.

The kid who once teamed with Michael Kidd-Gilchrist at St. Patrick's High School in New Jersey had already cashed in both on and off the court by his 24th birthday. His starring role as Uncle Drew in a viral campaign for Pepsi coupled with the launch of his signature Nike shoe, and other lucrative endorsement deals, helped make Irving one of the biggest corporate brands in the NBA. But as rival point guard Stephen Curry rose to dominance in the West, critics began to question Irving's durability and leadership while wondering aloud if his brand had become bigger than his actual game. Throughout the next six months that followed his therapeutic night in Washington, Irving would be under the microscope during a championship-or-bust mission for Cleveland.

Kyrie would pass all preliminary tests by closing the regular season with averages of 19.6 points and 4.7 assists. He'd also improve on his three-point field goal efficiency during the first three rounds of the playoffs—raising a career-low 32.1 percent in the regular season to well over 40 throughout the Cavs postseason run through the East. He'd return to the NBA Finals both healthy and productive, averaging over 23 points and five assists. But on the game's biggest stage, playing opposite the first unanimous MVP in NBA history, Irving would stumble again along his path to immortality. He shot 12-of-36 and finished with a combined plus/minus rating of –35 in the Cavaliers two humiliating losses, before overcoming the biggest obstacle in his young but storied career.

"I know that I can't play in-between or be indecisive, especially with guys in front of me," Irving said, following a 30-point performance that fueled a 120–90 Game 3 victory that proved to be the turning point of the series. "Just constantly in attack mode. I know my teammates consistently want me to do that, possession by possession, whether it's getting downhill or shooting jump shots or whatever it is."

Irving remained in attack mode, playing downhill and elevating his team to greatness while securing a come-from-behind Finals win. The point guard for the Cavaliers would lead Cleveland to its first championship in 52 years when most critics expected retreat. He'd also prove durable and worthy, while making the Vine videos, endorsement deals, and individual accolades a mere footnote on a basketball resume that now featured the game's greatest triumph.

Best PG in the Game

The next step for Kyrie Irving is to become considered the best point guard in the NBA. This is an extremely daunting challenge when considering that Stephen Curry, Russell Westbrook, and James Harden each play the point guard position. But as LeBron's relationship with Kyrie continues, that will be the goal that both players share. LeBron also knows that if he is going to experience the second half of a professional career filled with championships—like Michael Jordan, who won three rings after 31, and Kareem, who did damage for two separate decades—James will need Irving to remain elite. If James can continue to help Irving evolve from a consistency standpoint and also a body maintenance standpoint, it's possible that he could lead championship teams that LeBron is arguably the second best player on four or five years from today. What James invests in Irving will come back in the form of titles, or at least that seems to be the plan.

Kyrie Irving may never be considered the best point guard in the game, officially, but he did make the All-Star team again in 2017. This was his fourth trip to the ASG after missing the opportunity in 2016. But Irving is also only 25 years old and it stands to reason that he will make at least eight more trips to the All-Star game. If he is able to make at least three more after the 2017 appearance, he will have been an All-Star five times as LeBron's teammate. Only Dwyane Wade went to the All-Star game as LeBron's teammate more times than Irving would have in that scenario (Wade was an All-Star four times with LeBron and Kyrie has been an All-Star twice). If Kyrie can translate his All-Star game to at least one championship that he helps carry an old-aged LeBron toward winning, James could potentially retire with six rings to tie Mike before anybody ever notices he's about to accomplish as much. But this will rely on a veteran, a teacher, a mentor and a young superstar named Kyrie Irving to eventually turn such aspirations into reality.

Chapter 29

★ ★ ★

LeBron James
vs. Kobe Bryant

Kobe Bryant
Professional Career: 1996–2016
NBA: Los Angeles Lakers
Legacy Points: 111 (No. 5)

September 2015 marked the beginning of the end for Kobe Bryant. He would soon embark on a farewell tour through the NBA that was punctuated by a 60-point performance in his final professional game months later. But it wasn't easy. Bryant's injury-riddled body would suffer through one more 82-game grind—his 20th—as he waved goodbye to a game he loved and basketball community who loved him back.

Fans and players alike didn't want to believe it was ending. Even when he told us it was. That final voyage for the legendary Los Angeles Lakers superstar was scheduled to begin that September. Kobe's final NBA season was only a few weeks from tipping off when TMZ Sports caught up with 23-year-old NBA guard Dion Waiters.

The fourth-year pro was entering his second and final season with the Oklahoma City Thunder at the time. He would eventually play a supporting role in helping Kevin Durant and Russell Westbrook lead the Thunder to the Western Conference Finals before signing with the Miami Heat in 2016.

"Hey, do you play NBA 2K?" TMZ Sports asked Dion Waiters as he walked down a Los Angeles street in September of 2015 eating a popsicle.

"I play 2K and I play Madden," Waiters politely responds, in transit on foot from an off-season basketball workout to a waiting SUV driving him home.

"You know Kobe has his lowest rating ever in his career. He's rated 85," TMZ continues to announce to Waiters.

"*85?!*" Dion responds in dismay. "You gotta ask the Mamba about that."

"What do you think your rating is going to be?" TMZ asks the Syracuse product selected fourth overall in the 2012 NBA Draft.

"I ain't sure," Waiters replies.

"Do you think you should be rated higher than Kobe?" TMZ inquires.

"Hell no!" Dion responds emphatically. "That's the Bean, man."

The Bean from Philadelphia

Joseph Washington "Jellybean" Bryant graduated from John Bartram High School in Philadelphia, Pennsylvania, back in the early 1970s. Roughly four decades later, another young basketball prospect from Philly named Dion Waiters enrolled at John Bartram High for his ninth grade year. Instead of accepting a scholarship to Syracuse—like Waiters would do in 2010—Jellybean Bryant decided to continue his education and basketball career at nearby LaSalle University, where he blossomed into an NBA prospect with the Explorers.

The elder Bryant would be selected with the 14th overall pick in the 1975 NBA Draft, eventually landing back in his hometown as a professional. Joe was taken by the Golden State Warriors but later traded and signed by the Philadelphia 76ers. For the next four seasons, the 6'9" forward would appear in 287 regular season games for his hometown NBA team. Bryant averaged just under 15 minutes per night, playing alongside legends like Moses Malone and Julius Erving on teams that advanced to the playoffs.

In 1978, Joe and his wife, Pam Cox, would welcome a son into the world. Kobe Bean Bryant was born in Philadelphia. He'd spend time overseas as a child, watching his father conclude his pro career in Europe before the Bryant family returned home in 1992 so Kobe could attend high school in the States. He'd enroll at Lower Merion High School just outside of the city.

Kobe's Lower Merion Aces finished his freshman year in 1993 with a 4–20 varsity record. But the course of high school basketball history would be changed forever over the next three seasons. What Bryant accomplished, single-handedly— would become tales of lore and legend on playgrounds up and down the Mainline for decades to come. He was a basketball prodigy—a painter just dabbing his brush, from the city of Philadelphia.

Kobe helped his high school team compile a 77–13 record during his 10th, 11th, and 12th grade seasons at Lower Merion. He averaged over 30 points and 10 rebounds during that stretch. As a senior, R&B superstar Brandy accompanied Bryant to the prom. He'd then declare for the 1996 NBA Draft. As chronicled in Jonathan Abrams' tremendous book, *Boys Among Men*, Bryant would make that announcement in front of 400 students, coaches, teammates, media, and family in his high school gym.

Philly and Kobe

"When he lofted the MVP trophy after the West's 135–120 win, the boos rained down from the First Union Center as if he'd just stolen the Liberty Bell." Those words belong to a recap of the 2002 All-Star game offered by George Willis of the *New York Post*. He was describing Kobe Bryant's performance in front of his hometown Philadelphia fans as an NBA All-Star. They booed him—loudly.

The widely accepted narrative suggests those fans had not yet forgiven Bryant for his Los Angeles Lakers eliminating their 76ers the season before in the NBA Finals. So they booed him every time he touched the basketball.

The All-Star performance in Philadelphia was Bryant's fourth appearance on the NBA's midseason stage. Despite the boos, Kobe finished with 31 points, five assists, and five rebounds, while earning MVP honors for the game. He'd play in 15 All-Star games for his career—selected for 18—prior to retiring in 2016. But he never played in any of those All-Star games as a member of his hometown Sixers, and that meant something to the people of Philadelphia.

Kobe's Rings

On June 10, 2001, the Los Angeles Lakers traveled to the City of Brotherly Love as defending NBA champions. Shaq and Kobe had just captured their first ring the season before. After scoring only 15 points during a Game 1 loss in LA highlighted by Allen Iverson stepping over Lakers guard Tyronn Lue after a monster shot, Bryant responded with 31 points, eight rebounds, and six assists to even the series in Game 2.

In anticipation of the pivotal Game 3 matchup in Philly, Bryant told the fans of the team his father was playing for when he was born that he planned to cut their hearts out during the series. Which is exactly what he'd do. The Philly native led the visiting Lakers in scoring with 32 points during Game 3 of the 2002 NBA Finals. He also grabbed six boards and dished out three assists. His superstar teammate, Shaquille O'Neal, totaled 30 points while collecting 12 rebounds. By the end of the night, it was clear that Los Angeles was rolling again, and there wasn't anything that 35 points and 12 rebounds from the great Iverson could do about it.

Playing the best extended stretch of basketball of their careers together as a tandem at the time, peak Shaq and Kobe were unstoppable. O'Neal averaged 30.4 points and 15.4 rebounds in the postseason on the way to eliminating the 76ers in five games for their second straight title. Kobe, meanwhile, averaged 29.4 and 7.3—combining for roughly 60 points and 23 rebounds per night with Shaq. The Lakers would win a third-straight NBA championship the following season. Shaq and Kobe had solidified their place as one of the best one-two punches the NBA had ever seen—Two Batmans, no Robin.

Titles, Legacies, and Mike

Kobe won five NBA championships and Michael won six. The points, All-Star Games, on-court glare, competitive spirit, dedication to greatness, it was all a wash. Kobe was as close as we'll probably ever come again to Jordan in terms of everything he accomplished. What he did. The way he did it. The way you felt while he was doing it. There won't be another Kobe Bryant.

He inspired a generation that included LeBron James and many more.

"In high school I wore an Afro because of Kobe Bryant," James said. "Because he wore it. I wanted to be just like him, man. And I always said my inspiration came from [Michael] Jordan, but I always thought Jordan was so out of this world that I could never get there. Kobe was someone that I just always kind of wanted to be like and play like."

He won five and MJ won six. But how many could he have won if he played 10 more years with Shaq? The three championships that Los Angeles secured from

2000–02 is still the last three-peat in NBA history. But Shaq and Kobe could've maybe won six or even seven together over the course of their careers if they stayed together. They were two-man basketball at its very best. Inside and out, coming or going, they'd beat you however they wanted.

The most ironic aspect of the Shaq and Kobe break-up, however, is that both players wanted to carve their own legacies as leaders and legends of their own NBA franchise—exclusively. They each wanted it to be their Laker team, just as it was Jordan's Bulls. That's why the other guy didn't fit. But what they really needed was rings, which would've been easier to attain together.

Maybe they did need the divorce as Los Angeles Lakers teammates. Maybe we discredit teamwork too often in modern American sports, while choosing to elevate the individual while overlooking collective excellence. So maybe it did happen the only way it could. But no matter how it ended, there is no denying their greatness together. Arguably the best duo of all-time when they were at their collective peak, they were simply invincible.

Shaq won one more title with Dwyane Wade. Kobe won two more with Pau Gasol and Lamar Odom. Those meant something. But isn't it possible their individual talents would've shown through as teammates had they continued in LA? They put up numbers. They made All-Star teams. Signed endorsement deals. Became nationally known by only four letters. Won multiple championships. Shaq would finish with four, Kobe would finish with five.

Five NBA championships for the son of Joe "Jellybean" Bryant born to the city of Philadelphia as his father played alongside Dr. J. Five NBA championships for the kid from Philly who dared to do it his way and his way alone. Five NBA championships for the Bean.

LeBron vs. Kobe Bryant

Legacy Power Rankings: 97 vs. 111

Bryant:

- **MVP award:** 1 (7)
- **NBA championship:** 5 (50)
- **NBA All-Star:** 18 (54)

LeBron still has work to do to catch Kobe following his third championship. He's not past him yet. It's really strange that Kobe Bryant only won one MVP award during his NBA career. But even if it were locker room squabbles and off the court issues that possibly hurt his relationship with media members who were voting, the fact remains that Bryant only won one MVP and James has already won four.

Heading into the 2016–17 NBA season, LeBron trails Kobe by 14 Legacy Points. He needs a fourth NBA championship (10 points) and two All-Star appearances (6) to surpass Bryant for No. 4 overall. Other scenarios to total 14 or more Legacy Points are certainly attainable in our estimation for James as well to eventually pass Bryant by the time he retires. It will be an epic run to get there, but we expect James to make that climb in his second act.

Chapter 30

★ ★ ★

Evolution of LeBron: Kevin Love Effect

Kevin Love was formally introduced as a member of the Cleveland Cavaliers on August 26, 2014. Two years earlier, he stood alongside LeBron James on a court in London with an American Flag draped across his shoulders and a gold medal dangling from his neck. Upon his return to Northeast Ohio, the first call James made was to his Olympic teammate, asking Love to join the fight in Cleveland. The All-Star power forward from the Minnesota Timberwolves would agree to a trade that finalized the union soon after.

LeBron James and Kevin Love first became friends in the sense that each was a franchise player and superstar in the NBA, and each had developed a respect for one another during their time as teammates with USA Basketball. James marveled at Love's skill set, which for his size as a legit center at the time in the League, is incredibly developed from a dribble, pass, and most importantly shoot standpoint. Throughout Love's time in the NBA, he'd evolve from first a traditional big from UCLA (which produced superstars like Kareem Abdul-Jabbar and Bill Walton at the center position before him) to a stretch four who could create mismatch issues while spreading the floor with his three-point ability. The latter reason made Love the type of scoring big that Chris Bosh made famous in Miami. But the transition for Love, like Bosh, would not be instantaneously gratifying for all involved as Kevin and LeBron set out on their journey together heading into the 2014–15 season.

The marriage between Love, James, Kyrie, and the Cavaliers would eventually deliver a championship less than 24 months after the former Minnesota Timberwolves big man agreed to a trade to The Land. But in order to maximize the collective talent of the triumvirate along the way—an effort that seemed to take even bigger strides forward after the Cavs secured their first title in franchise history—Love would be asked to make sacrifices most NBA players of his stature would never consider.

He arrived in Cleveland as a three-time All-Star, All-NBA player, and regarded by some as the best power forward in the game. For the Cavaliers to ultimately succeed as a team, however, Love would be forced to reinvent that all-world game entirely. Instead of being the focal point of pass-first point guard Ricky Rubio and his T-Wolves offense, Love would be forced to find his shots from the perimeter—whenever the ball was able to trickle his way from LeBron and Kyrie.

Love's ability and willingness to make the changes he did as an individual player and still perform at an elite level—a level that eventually earned him an All-Star berth in 2017 for the first time since arriving from the Twin Cities—is the primary reason Cleveland's Big Three was able to succeed as a unit and secure the 2016 championship. It's also something often overlooked when it comes to the narrative surrounding the supremely versatile Love, whose ability to adapt and alter his game made it look easier than it actually was.

For six seasons in Minnesota, the player who was drafted as a 20-year-old center out of college in 2008 averaged 19.2 points and 12.2 rebounds. Everything ran through Love offensively, and he always knew when and where his touches would come. He'd attempt 53.8 percent of his field goals from areas 10 feet away from the basket and in for the Timberwolves, with only 23.6 percent of his shots coming from three-point range. But the winning recipe in Cleveland required a different ingredient.

The Chris Bosh Prophecy

NBA All-Star forward and champion Chris Bosh publicly warned Kevin Love about how challenging the adjustment alongside two ball-dominant superstars like LeBron and Kyrie would actually be for him as a player. Like Love would

LeBron high fives Kyrie Irving and Kevin Love during a 2016 game against the Hornets.
(Sam Sharpe-USA TODAY Sports)

experience in Cleveland, it is very difficult to transition from the franchise player who coaches designed plays to get them the best scoring opportunities possible to the third wheel of a Big Three scoring unit—even if it is an All-NBA unit. Kyrie and LeBron are looking to score the basketball first more times than not. They are also essentially the only Cleveland players who bring the ball up and initiate offense. Furthermore, to be at their best—like LeBron and Wade with Bosh—James and Irving need the floor spread so they can attack the basket. Love was already an All-Star, but he was asked to be a specific type of All-Star in Cleveland and he would help deliver a ring in response.

Besides his total field goal attempts going down alongside James and Irving, Love was asked to primarily use his shot-making ability from the perimeter to open driving lanes for his teammates by dragging opposing bigs away from the basket and create more of those driving lanes that James and Irving thrived on. His paint touches decreased significantly as a result, as Love attempted 45 percent of his field goals from three-point range and only 36 percent from 10 feet and in for the Cavs by year two. That transition wasn't always easy, especially on a team where the two primary ball-handlers are also its two leading scorers. But as the 2015–16 campaign wore on, Love began to hit his stride at just the right time. He'd average 16 points and 9.9 rebounds during the regular season before turning in his best stretch of basketball as a Cavalier when his team and city needed it most.

Love Helps Deliver Illusive Title

Despite averaging 18.9 points and 12.5 rebounds during the first eight games of the postseason, Love's critics would never be louder than they were during the Eastern Conference Finals. In each of the Cavaliers two losses to the Toronto Raptors, he struggled to score only 6.5 points per night while shooting a combined 21.7 percent from the floor. He was admittedly awful during those two games, but responded by averaging 22.5 points and seven rebounds in the next two on 61.9 percent shooting to secure a berth in the NBA Finals. He'd then open Game 1 against the Golden State Warriors with 17 and 13 before helping Cleveland defeat a team with the best regular-season record in NBA history in dramatic fashion.

"I really just focused on getting on the glass," Love said, about stretches of the season when his scoring opportunities and numbers dipped. "Rebounding can be something constant for me even when I have an off shooting night."

Love would remain a constant force in all areas of the game throughout the Finals. As they concluded, standing on a court alongside LeBron James once again—this time draped in the glow of an NBA championship—all the sacrifices Love made for his team had paid off. He had helped secure an elusive title that first appeared possible on the August day he arrived in Cleveland, and allowed a city to celebrate such a victory for the first time in 52 years.

An All-Star is Reborn

The first season as LeBron's teammate was rocky for Kevin Love. It was also rocky for Chris Bosh. He went from averaging 26.1 points per game for Minnesota in 2014 to wrapping up the 2015 regular season scoring only 16.4 per night for Cleveland. His rebounding numbers—now standing behind the three-point line when shots go up that he used to be positioned in the paint to collect—also dipped from 12.5 to 9.7 in his first year with the Cavs. But by the end of his second season, amidst constant trade rumors, Love looked increasingly comfort-able on his way to similar numbers. After his first postseason run alongside James was cut short due to an injury suffered in the first round against the Celtics, Love averaged 15 points and nine rebounds while defending Stephen Curry into a miss late in Game 7 to help seal the victory. Then, in his third season, with the weight of lost championships over five decades lifted from he and his teammates shoulders, Love has thus far improved his numbers to 20 points and 11 rebounds per game and was named an All-Star once again.

Kevin Love and Chris Bosh should be used as examples to illustrate how spe-cifically hard it is to blend your talents alongside two ball-dominant superstars in today's NBA. The transition is easier for players like James or Wade or Irving who will be handling the ball for just about the same amount of time either way. But Love and Bosh were necessary ingredients in each of LeBron's championships runs. It takes a special teammate and a special person to not only be willing to make the sacrifices they made for the betterment of the team, but also be skilled enough to actually do that effectively in an NBA game. Love is talented and he's a better teammate that he's ever been credited for. He may be in trade rumors for the rest of his career, but as long as he's playing alongside LeBron and continuing to get better there is no reason to think that Love will not continue to help James stack rings in Cleveland for years to come under the direction of coach Tyronn Lue and the Cavs.

Chapter 31

★ ★ ★

LeBron James vs. Kareem Abdul-Jabbar

Kareem Abdul-Jabbar
Professional Career: 1969–89
NBA: Milwaukee Bucks, Los Angeles Lakers
Legacy Points: 159 (No. 4)

Is he better than Kareem, Russell, or Jordan? That's what I asked my father in response to his signature facial expression that politely suggested this list I had explained may now have been rendered useless upon further inspection. He was the first person I detailed the Legacy Points to from a ranking standpoint. Best player in your league at least once, point system, Kareem, Russell, and Jordan at the top. He was with me the whole way. Makes sense for LeBron to move up the legacy ranks, too. He liked it, said it was cool and rationale. But he really did not appreciate Jerry West being omitted.

"Wait—Jerry West is not on your Legacy Power Rankings list?"

"No. He never won an MVP."

"He *never* won an MVP?"

"No, runner-up four times though."

"Four times runner-up? I'm pretty sure you need to count that."

But is he better than Kareem, Russell, or Jordan?

The Legacy Power Rankings goal is to identify the four, five greatest players of all-time—or however many more as basketball continues to evolve and thrive for generations to come—who are in that specific GOAT conversation. While this MVP-exclusive list certainly omits iconic legends who probably deserved to be considered their league's most valuable at least once as players over many decades—like West, John Havlicek, Elgin Baylor, Patrick Ewing, Jason Kidd, or Dwyane Wade—it does feature Kareem, Russell, and Jordan among the top three spots, alongside Kobe, Duncan, Shaq, and others in the Top 10.

From 1958 to 1998, Russell, Kareem, and Jordan, for example, combined to win 17 NBA MVP awards. They also accounted for 23 NBA championships and carried the sport of basketball forward throughout the decades. From skyhooks to paint defense and free throw line dunks, Kareem, Russell and Jordan will always live among basketball's most iconic heroes for as long as the sport is played. To enter the conversation alongside Kareem Abdul-Jabbar is a Herculean task.

Heaven Was Alcindor's Playground

The great Rick Telander mentions the name of a young New York City high school superstar named Lew Alcindor for the first time on page 64 of his literary ground-breaking masterpiece *Heaven Is A Playground*. The book, published in 1976 after the author spent a summer chronicling playground basketball in New York City, pushes not just the idea that these stories are an aspect of basketball's rich history, but also offers a level of nuanced detail that illustrates how playgrounds like these in New York helped develop the individual games of basketball's greatest players while detailing the lives of Rodney Parker, Fly Williams, Albert King, and others.

In a postscript penned by Telander, which was included in a 1988 re-publication of the book, he references the big city influence over basketball beginning to fade as the 1990s approach. The Eastern NBA All-Star team included Isiah Thomas, Michael Jordan, Dominique Wilkins, Larry Bird, Moses Malone, Danny Ainge, and Patrick Ewing as a reference that year. The West rolled out Magic Johnson, Fat Lever, Alex English, Karl Malone, Hakeem Olajuwon, Clyde Drexler, and Kareem Abdul-Jabbar, among others.

From *Heaven is a Playground* by Rick Telander:

"Drugs—cocaine and its derivatives, particularly—have changed the structure of urban American society. They also have changed the city game. At its highest levels, basketball is still a black man's game—22 out of the 25 players in last February's NBA All-Star game were black—but it is more and more the suburban and small-town game as well. In that recent All-Star Game only eight athletes came from large cities, while 17 came from towns such as Leeds, Alabama; Summerfield, Louisiana; French Lick, Indiana. Six players came from rural Carolinas, while only prehistoric Kareem Abdul-Jabbar represented the very cradle of the city game, New York City."

Kareem was selected with the No. 1 pick overall in 1969 after starring at UCLA for the great John Wooden. He'd win an NBA championship for the Milwaukee Bucks who drafted him, as well as an MVP in 1971 while representing Milwaukee in six-straight All-Star games. The young center had previously won 71 straight games playing New York City high school basketball for Power Memorial, before winning three straight NCAA championships for Coach Wooden's Bruins. The NYC kid born in 1947 would rise from the playgrounds to take over the basketball world with Skyhooks, dunks, dimes and all-around winning play as a superstar teammate for two decades in the League.

Exploratory Legacy of Greatness

"You hear a name like Kareem," LeBron James told Cleveland.com after passing Jabbar on the all-time scoring list. "He's a guy who's done so many great things, not only as an individual but as a teammate, winning championships in the '80s and things of that nature and how many points he's put up— he's somebody you read about. I didn't get an opportunity to actually watch him play growing up, but I just read about his accomplishments and things he was able to do."

The legendary basketball player who patented a move we'd call the "Skyhook" was awarded the Presidential Medal of Freedom by Barack Obama in 2016 for the barriers he'd continue to threaten during life after basketball. The NBA's All-Time leading scorer would go on to become a *New York Times* best-selling author and columnist, writing for *Time Magazine* and other outlets while authoring over 15 books. He'd appear in films with Bruce Lee, as well as famously playing a pilot in a timeless classic named *Airplane!*.

Kareem demonstrates a level of greatness that suggests there is more for us all to explore after we conquer one arena of our life and move to the next. He won his first MVP in 1971 and his sixth in 1980. He was an All-Star every year except one from 1970 to '79, while winning one NBA championship during that stretch that spanned 11 seasons. This would be a Hall of Fame career in itself for Abdul-Jabbar, if not for winning five more NBA championships from 1980 to 1989 during the NBA three-point era. He'd bring the game of Russell and Chamberlain as far as the big man could take it, before Jordan helped usher in the modern brand of NBA basketball at the conclusion of Kareem's legendary career.

Jordan would win his first NBA championship for the Chicago Bulls in 1991. He'd win his first MVP in 1988, and second in 1991 after Kareem retired from the game following a celebratory tour through the regular season that honored his career at every stop. The Laney High product from Wilmington, North Carolina, would take over the NBA from there, as the torch was officially passed to the next generation of superstar from the best player New York City high school basketball has ever seen. Abdul-Jabbar published his first book, titled *Kareem*, in 1994. He'd offer other biographical writings, while launching a fictional series called *Streetball Crew* along with the *Mycroft Holmes* series and other creative writing formats he continues to explore as he inspires us all to train our minds as well as our bodies throughout all of our lives.

Showtime Lakers

Kareem Abdul-Jabbar may never be considered the single greatest player in NBA history. But, he always deserves to be mentioned in the conversation for his statistical accomplishments alone. Abdul-Jabbar technically ranks No. 2 in Legacy Points with 157. He is ranked behind Jordan in the NBA legends section of this book, as well as Bill Russell. But one of the biggest reasons for why Kareem always deserves to be mentioned in the conversation of single greatest player of all-time, beyond those statistical claims, is this:

More than maybe any other player in history, the totality and evolution of Kareem's game transcends all eras the best. His style of play would work in today's game: he could run, he could play in the half-court and he could bang with anybody inside. There is no era that Kareem would not dominate and that includes the next 30 years of NBA basketball from here.

Abdul-Jabbar was an NBA center who exceeded lofty expectations with John Wooden and his UCLA Bruins by winning three straight NCAA championships. He won MVPs and NBA championships in the early 1970s as a traditional Russell, Chamberlain-type center, and then again while running with Magic Johnson and high-flying, fast-breaking Showtime Lakers of the late 1980s. Playing as a mobile big man who can run the break effectively with a nice touch 10–12 feet from the basket never gets old. Kareem could beat you like the traditional giants or by running the floor. There wasn't anything he couldn't do.

Pat Riley's Showtime Lakers would win the NBA championship in 1987 and 1988. They would represent rings No. 5 and 6 for the 1970 Rookie of the Year named Abdul-Jabbar. While playing in 158 regular season games during his final two championship runs, Kareem averaged 30 minutes per contest. He scored 16 points per game during that stretch while collecting 6.3 rebounds. In 42 postseason games from 1987 to '88, he scored 17 or more points 17 times during the Showtime Lakers championship runs. He also grabbed at least seven rebounds in 16 of those memorable NBA playoff games.

During the two-year reign of Magic Johnson, Kareem Abdul-Jabbar and the Showtime Lakers, the 19-time All-Star center averaged 16.3 points and six rebounds per game. He scored 32 points, grabbed six rebounds, and blocked four shots to close out the Celtics during a 13-point Lakers win in 1987. Abdul-Jabbar would also give the Pistons 26 and six during Game 5 of the Finals the following season. Kareem was 41 years and 66 days old when he helped his Lakers secure his sixth championship two games later.

LeBron vs. Kareem Abdul-Jabbar

Legacy Power Rankings: 97 vs. 159
Abdul-Jabbar:
- **MVP award: 6 (42)**
- **NBA championship: 6 (60)**
- **NBA All-Star: 19 (57)**

Following his 2016 NBA championship in Cleveland, LeBron would need to close his career in a similar manner to Kareem to actually catch Abdul-Jabbar. The 1970 ROY would close his second decade from 1980 to '89 by winning five NBA titles (50), one MVP (7), and appearing in 10 straight-All-Star games (30) for a total of 87 Legacy Points. But when does

LeBron's final 10 seasons begin? Did they start already? He'd need 62 Legacy Points to catch Kareem from his spot at No. 9 overall with 97—or three more championships (30), two MVPs (14), and six more All-Star appearances starting in 2018 to get to 159.

While we don't expect LeBron to total more points than Abdul-Jabbar, we do believe he dominates a changing game, just as Kareem carried the game Russell and Chamberlain to Magic and Michael. But Kareem Abdul-Jabbar is a Muslim American hero who has been recognized by the highest levels of the United States government for the life he continues to live both on and off the floor regardless of where his basketball achievements officially slot him. He is never satisfied and never content. He continues to push himself, continues to question, continues to lead. His culture, his people, and his sport have been left with an indelible mark based on all Kareem's accomplished, taking the city's game to places it never imagined when he first started bouncing the ball on the blacktops of New York City.

Chapter 32

★ ★ ★

Evolution of LeBron: Tristan, J.R., and Mike Effect

Tristan Thompson

Tristan Thompson's NBA career will be forever linked in multiple aspects with LeBron James legacy as a professional basketball player and business icon. The most obvious way the two Cavaliers teammates are forever linked is in the championship they helped deliver to Cleveland. But besides stepping up with his legendary consistency and work ethic to deliver big minutes in the NBA Finals, Thompson will go down as the first Lottery selection to win an NBA championship for the team that drafted him in Klutch Sports history as an Agency. When LeBron's business associate, Rich Paul, who repped LeBron at that point in his career, departed with Creative Arts Agency, Thompson was the first CAA athlete to declare that he'd join Paul and James at Klutch. That decision would have a rippling effect, as many others selected at the top of the draft would follow Tristan to Klutch.

Based on these ties with Paul, dating back to his days as an NBA prospect for the Texas Longhorns in the Big 12, LeBron's relationship with Tristan dates as far back as his debut in 2011 alongside fellow rookie, Kyrie Irving. Serving as a first a mentor, then friend and teammate, LeBron watched from Miami as Thompson took the floor for Cleveland on February 10, 2012, a 20-year-old rookie from Toronto, Ontario, who'd collect 13 rebounds during a 113–112 loss to the Milwaukee Bucks. Four games later, the fourth Canadian-born player to ever be named to the McDonald's All-American Game posted the first double-double of his NBA career with 15 and 12 during a 93–92 win over the Sacramento Kings. Nearly five years and more than 3,000 rebounds later, Thompson's heart, energy and production has remained more of a constant than anyone could've ever imagined when Chris Grant used a controversial selection to make the pride of Canada his fourth overall pick of the 2011 draft.

Two weeks after his 25th birthday, Thompson posted the 113th double-double of his Cavaliers career while playing in his 362nd consecutive NBA game dating back to that night in early February of 2012. The appearance broke a franchise record set by the great Jim Chones that had stood for more than 40 years. He'd extend his streak of consistency and reliability to 370 straight appearances during his second season as LeBron's teammate heading into the 2016 playoffs. It would be there, on basketball's biggest stage, that Tristan would prove to be flawless during a Game 6 Finals matchup with the Golden State Warriors when his team could ill-afford anything less. During that Game 6 performance from Thompson, the 6'9" forward defended throughout the half-court, set game-changing screens, and made all six of his field-goal attempts to finish with 15 points and 16 rebounds to help LeBron send the series back to Oakland for Game 7 and a chance to deliver Cleveland its first championship in 52 years.

See Ball, Get Ball

"For me, my approach is simple," Tristan Thompson once told *SLAM* magazine of his role alongside LeBron James, Kyrie Irving, and Kevin Love for the Cavaliers. "I call it, 'See ball, get ball.' I am going to put myself in a position on the court to rebound the basketball well for our team, then finish around the rim while also making an impact defensively."

Thompson matched a season high by collecting 16 boards during the 43 minutes of tireless execution that helped his Cavaliers force Game 7. He saw the ball, and used every ounce of his being to get the ball, grabbing 13 or more rebounds in each of Cleveland's first three Finals victories. His accomplishments may always be met with revisionist historians who remind us that Klay Thompson and Kawhi Leonard were still on the draft board the night Tristan first became a Cavalier. But the only thing we now know is that the 2016 Cavs would not have won Cleveland its first championship in franchise history without the kid born north of Lake Erie.

"Like LeBron and Kyrie said, be a star in your role," Thompson said following the victory that evened the NBA Finals at 3–3. "Be a star in your role, and for me that's high energy, use my motor, just play hard. Play hard, be relentless on the glass. And that's what I bring to this team. That's my job, just be a star in your role, and I try to do that every night."

Tristan Thompson truly is and was a star in his role during his first three seasons as a teammate of LeBron's. Besides stepping up in the 2016 Finals, Tristan was also a critical reason why the injury-riddled Cavaliers were able to extend Golden State to six games with his performance on both ends of the floor in 2015. He's a perfect fit for today's NBA and positions LeBron with depth up front needed to win championships by Thompson's ability to guard both the screener and the ball-handler while extending the pick-and-roll to allow a help defender to arrive. He is the type of defensive big that James needs to bring off the bench, and is always working to improve offensively. For as long as LeBron James is a player for the Cleveland Cavaliers, Tristan Thompson will be on his roster for all the reasons referenced above and many more.

General Manager LeBron

Tristan Thompson deserves as much money as Cleveland Cavaliers owner Dan Gilbert is willing to pay him. But it would not be entirely accurate to suggest that LeBron and his status as the NBA's best player, combined with his relationship to Rich and how important Tristan was to their agency from a loyalty standpoint early on, did not help Thompson earn his $82 million contract. It looks like a steal now after the great free agency summer heist of 2016 as the NBA salary cap number exploded, but it also was hard to imagine that Tristan would earn nearly $20 million per season while watching his first and second and third seasons for the lowly Cavs. But everything lined up exactly right for Thompson, and he never stopped working hard. That effort and work ethic was met with millions. As long as the checks clear, in my opinion, Thompson is worth every penny. But that still doesn't mean this was one of the first times that LeBron, the player, was able to use his leverage as the franchise player to earn maybe more money for his friend, teammate, and business associate than Tristan may have earned otherwise.

The Tristan Thompson contract could be viewed as somewhat of a win for LeBron James the businessman. While the truth was certainly never this, in many ways LeBron came back to the egotistical owner who wrote nasty things about him and played hard to earn this owner more money. The Tristan Thompson deal, however, was clearly LeBron holding Gilbert over the coals and forcing him to pay Thompson as much money as the NBA would allow. This was whether he or his talent evaluators valued Thompson as an $80 million player or not. This move, and subsequent contracts with Klutch athlete J.R. Smith as well as others, helped send a message to the billionaire class in America that LeBron was coming for the top spot. James was essentially the first player in NBA history to figure out how he and a sports agency he founded could not only earn money off his friends and teammates contracts, but also force his teams to pay those player the most money possible.

Friends and Teammates

Despite their personal relationships, Thompson, like all players his age, gave LeBron the respect his NBA championships and MVPs would require when they first teamed up in 2014. But much like Chris Bosh, Thompson has emerged through two NBA Finals appearances and one NBA championship as a player who is willing and able to call LeBron out on the court or in the huddle during games if the moment requires. This dynamic as teammates, combined with Tristan's universal respect and love up and down the roster, is something that helps keep a superstar like James engaged in the team dynamic more than he might tend to be if there weren't teammates who could challenge him on the roster. If a teammate has something LeBron should potentially know about, Tristan's close relationship with LeBron helps merge those avenues by being approachable by all involved.

As a rebounder and versatile defender, Thompson is the type of player that NBA teams traditionally win championships with as a fifth starter or key reserve off the bench. The fact that Tristan can do this on a nightly basis while playing over 350 straight games makes him even more important for championship-caliber teams. But for Tristan to be the player he naturally is as a competitor, and also has such a healthy and deep relationship with LeBron makes him a truly special teammate. He's a poor man's version of what Dennis Rodman was for a time for Michael Jordan, but with a much better attitude based more in reality than the great Rodman was during his time in Chicago. Thompson has always fit the Cleveland work ethic and mentality for the city built on such attributes. When James arrived, he simply fit perfectly alongside him too. Along the way, the first two Klutch athletes in NBA history have raised at least one banner together for the Cavaliers. By the time they are finished, expect even more championship stories with multiple chapters filled by the exploits of Tristan Trevor Thompson from Canada.

J.R. Smith

J.R. Smith stood on a stage alongside his daughter and teammate LeBron James to speak about his support for Democratic Presidential Candidate Hillary Clinton. Despite winning the popular vote, Clinton lost the election, but not before Earl Joseph "J.R." Smith III stepped forward as an American success story to voice his opinion on the presidential stage. It marked a long journey from a young prep to pros player who was labeled a malcontent and locker room cancer early on his career, to now a public figure who was respected enough by the Democratic nominee to join her on stage. Since arriving via trade from the New York Knicks during LeBron's first season back in Cleveland, Smith proved to be the consummate professional deserving of such honors. He brought his daughter on stage to join him, after chronicling her journey through civics class on Instagram, and he helped show us all what's possible when we look inward and ask ourselves how we can all become the best versions of ourselves.

J.R. Smith deserves credit for becoming the man he did both on and off the court alongside James as a 30-year-old who learned from his mistakes early on. But LeBron deserves credit for the J.R. Smith renaissance that played out in Cleveland too. For as much progress as he made personally, the issues that plagued Smith first in Denver and then in New York were certainly his fault in many respects. But J.R. knew he had an opportunity to do something special with LeBron and he did what was required to be a part of that championship success. What made it the most special for Cavs and NBA fans, however, was that Smith became that starting shooting guard piece of an NBA championship game simply by bringing out the very best aspects of who he always was as a player.

The J.R. Smith Role

The kid they called J.R. was born to let it fly. As the shooting guard for the 2015–16 Cleveland Cavaliers, Smith flourished in a role that required him to be exactly himself. But it wasn't always this natural for the 13-year NBA veteran who entered the League directly out of St Benedict's Prep in Newark, New Jersey. After being named co-MVP alongside Dwight Howard of the 2004 McDonald's All-American Game, Smith was drafted with the 18th pick overall by the New Orleans Hornets. He'd make two more professional stops as a member of the Denver Nuggets and New York Knicks before finding a home that seemed crafted specifically for Smith by the basketball gods.

With a smile on his face, the player once labeled as trouble for locker rooms throughout the Association thrived in Cleveland as teammates with LeBron. Smith also graciously welcomed the directive from coach Tyronn Lue to fire away at all costs whenever he was open. Whether he was falling down, had a hand in his face, or was stepping into an open look in transition, the Cavaliers needed Smith to be a consistent weapon from beyond the arc and that's specifically what he became. During a game against the Milwaukee Bucks on April 5, 2016, he'd ceremoniously fulfill that mission by knocking down seven triples to set the Cavs franchise record for most three-pointers made in a single season. It is a franchise record that Smith currently holds through the 2017 NBA All-Star Game as he continues to inflate his total with triple after triple for the Cavs.

"I think it was the third one, honestly," Smith said while colorfully describing the moment he believed he caught fire during the 39-point win over the Bucks when he set the franchise three-point record just prior to the 2016 playoffs. "When I shot it, I felt a little bit off-balance but I just held my follow-through and it kind of rimmed in. After that, it felt like all of them were going down."

Smith would finish the 2016 regular season shooting 40 percent from three while knocking down a record-setting 204 triples. Those totals were also good for seventh in the NBA overall in three-pointers made and 21st in efficiency. But Smith was not simply a three-point specialist. At multiple times during the season, Coach Lue used his postgame press conference to refer to Smith as "the best on-ball defender" on the team. But it was his brash delivery from three-point range that helped provide the biggest spark along the Cavaliers run to immortality.

"Everybody keeps telling me to keep shooting," Smith said as the Cavaliers postseason run approached. "Everybody is enthused, especially the guys on the bench. I think we're feeding off a great energy coming into the playoffs and we're understanding who we are and what type of team we need to be. We're always looking to get better, I can't say we are there yet, but we're close. So we'll see what we can do."

During the Cavaliers march to the 2016 NBA championship, it was more of the same from Smith as he offered a dizzying performance from deep on a routine basis. He hit seven three-pointers in Game 2 against the Detroit Pistons, and seven more in Game 2 against the Atlanta Hawks. Heading into the NBA Finals matchup with the Golden State Warriors, Smith had connected on 49-of-106 three-point field goals to lead the Cavaliers in that category through 14 games. He'd also improve his efficiency to a stifling 46 percent. The player who was initially perceived as a risky asset forced upon David Griffin in a trade with the Knicks for an opportunity to acquire Iman Shumpert had become the long-range assassin Cleveland needed to secure its first championship in 52 years. Then he never wore a shirt for about a month, and president Barack Obama would go as far as thanking J.R. for wearing a shirt to the White House following the championship celebration in Cleveland.

Spacing the Floor for LeBron

Soon after Delonte West and later Mo Williams arrived in Cleveland prior to LeBron's departure in 2010, the NBA world collectively realized the way to best construct a team around James. For many decades of NBA basketball, rosters were built from the inside out. They first started with centers like Bill Russell, Wilt Chamberlain, Kareem Abdul-Jabbar, and others, and added guards and wings as complementary pieces around those giants. Magic Johnson's Lakers featured Kareem up front. Larry Bird's Celtics offered Robert Parish, and Jordan's Bulls bucked tradition by running Phil Jackson's triangle. The triangle was also what helped Shaquille O'Neal and Kobe Bryant win three straight championships for Los Angeles under Phil. But the changing NBA that James entered as a rookie in 2003 took time to figure out how to best build around James. Or at least, it took the Cavs until LeBron's return to really round out that type of roster, which features shooters all over the floor to create spacing for driving lanes.

Smith is one of the best floor spacers that LeBron every played with who is not going to the Hall of Fame. Ray Allen is that HOFer, and certainly a better three-point shooter than Smith. But while James Jones and Mike Miller were elite floor spacers as well, Smith's raw aggressiveness made him one of the most dangerous long-range assassins and floor spacers that LeBron ever played with. What makes J.R. special and deadly is that he doesn't care if he misses, that will never deter him from firing. And as long as LeBron is telling him to shoot, that's more than enough reason for him to find a place along the arc to seek out his next shot. But along with hitting more three-pointers than any Cavaliers player to ever play for the franchise, Smith is a perfect fit alongside LeBron. Besides knocking down triples he also uses his athleticism to defend.

When the shots are falling, Smith has the ability to perform like an elite defender. His friendship with James would lead him to sign with Klutch Sports and join teammate Tristan Thompson as players for Richard Paul's agency along with LeBron. That decision, combined with J.R.'s emergence as a championship player who was among the best three-point shooters in the League, would help Smith cash in on a lucrative free agent deal to remain in Cleveland after the title. He allowed LeBron to become his friend and help him improve. As a result, Smith helped James win one championship and maybe more before he hangs up his six-shooter.

Mike Miller

Narratives sometimes suggest that LeBron James and Mike Miller don't have all that much in common. Miller grew up in the Dakotas before starring for an NCAA championship contender under the direction of head coach Billy Donavon at Florida. James, meanwhile, spent part of his childhood growing up in Akron's inner city before jumping straight from high school to the pros. One is white and one is black, but both are tall and both could ball in the League from Day 1. Miller was named the NBA's Rookie of the Year while LeBron was still in high school. But James would eventually earn that same honor in 2003, and roughly 10 years after that he'd win an NBA title with the Miami Heat alongside Miller.

The Miami Heat signed a 30-year-old shooting guard entering his 10th NBA season when they acquired the sharpshooting Miller in 2010. While battling injuries for much of the next three seasons, Miller would shoot over 41 percent from three-point range during 139 appearances for the Heat through the conclusion of the 2013 season. Miller would help James to his first and second NBA championships by spacing the floor with one of the best three-point strokes in NBA history from a mechanical standpoint.

The let-it-fly extraordinaire topped out on South Beach at 45.3 percent from distance during the first of LeBron's two title years in Miami. During the playoffs, Miller shot over 42 percent from three-point range over a 40-game stretch that saw James, Wade, Bosh, Miller, and the Miami Heat bring home two titles. He went 6-for-6 from three-point range in his first game of the 2011–12 campaign on January 17 after returning from early season injury. Miller would finish the year by nailing 7-of-8 threes to help LeBron and company close out Kevin Durant, Russell Westbrook, James Harden, and the Oklahoma City Thunder in Game 5 of the 2012 NBA Finals.

Miller's lifelong dedication to the long-range shot has made an impact on LeBron's game as a player ever since their time together. When James broke into the League, the only thing remotely broken about his game was his three-point shot. LeBron shot 29 percent from three as a rookie. He then finished each of his next five seasons by shooting 35 percent, 34, 32, 32, 34 and 33. During LeBron's first season as Mike Miller's teammate he shot only 33 percent. But in their second season on South Beach together, James' three-point field goal efficiency slowly started to rise. James wrapped up the 2012 campaign by improving to then career-high of 36 percent from deep.

As he secured back-to-back rings with Miller, LeBron then improved even more, to 40.6 percent from deep. The extra hours he spent working out with Mike, watching Mike shoot and talking about shooting with his expert marksman of a teammate slowly helped LeBron expand his game beyond the perimeter. While winning his fourth MVP and third NBA championship, James used that 41 percent stroke from deep to help him post averages of 27, eight, and seven. It was the deadliest version of LeBron the NBA had ever seen. The wet jumper he seemed to also now possess would prove to be a big reason for that overall improvement of a reigning champion.

The Champ and Mike

It's hard to mention Mike Miller as a member of the Miami Heat and not also mention the teammate they all call Champ. James Jones was part of that effort alongside Miller to help push LeBron's game beyond the arc efficiently. Miller and Jones would battle for hours in search of the perfect shot. LeBron would watch or join or both, which improved the way he approached his performance as a shooter. It's also hard to deny the fact that he improved from 29 percent as a rookie to 41 percent roughly 10 years later. The time spent next to Jones and Miller helped develop that aspect of James' game while also playing critical roles on each of LeBron's first title runs. But beyond the numbers, Miller was a teammate like Jones that LeBron trusted. He'd ask both Champ and Mike to come with him and build a championship culture once again in Cleveland.

Mike Miller would be signed by the Denver Nuggets as LeBron finally cashed in his NBA championship for Cleveland in 2016. By that time, Miller had won two titles with James and made a trip back to a third NBA Finals in 2015 with Cleveland. Even while away in Denver, Miller not only kept close tabs on his former teammates in Cleveland, he also kept his family living year round in Northeast Ohio and attending the same schools they did when he first arrived in Cleveland with LeBron. One of the very first Instagram posts that LeBron would share on social media after signing with the Cavaliers in 2014 was of him and Miller in the gym at Akron SVSM working on their outside shot. Let it fly was included in the caption, because that's what LeBron's teammate Mike Miller always seemed to do at just the right time.

Miller's Amnesty and the Return

The Miami Heat used their amnesty decision on Mike Miller following the 2013 NBA championship. He was released with full pay while still able to sign with another team, but removed simply for salary cap reasons almost exclusively. But while the Heat were within their rights to use their amnesty on Miller at that point in his career, the decision never sat well with James. During LeBron's final season in Miami, Miller signed on to appear in 82 games for the Memphis Grizzlies. He logged over 1,700 minutes during the regular season and shot 46 percent from the floor as Miami eventually lost in the NBA Finals.

Owner Micky Arison and Team President Pat Riley's decision to amnesty Miller was offered in several reports as reason for LeBron's growing discontent with the Miami franchise. Whether that's true or not, LeBron did then leave the franchise as soon as he was able to. Miller, also, ended up reuniting with LeBron before moving on to play for the Denver Nuggets through 2017.

Chapter 33

★ ★ ★

LeBron James vs. Bill Russell

Bill Russell
Professional Career: 1956–1969
NBA: Boston Celtics
Legacy Points: 181 (No.3)

Boston Celtics Hall of Famer and the NBA's most innovative champion, Bill Russell, along with his wife, Rose, were prominent members of the Civil Rights Movement in the United States less than 60 years ago during the 1960s. The Celtics center, whose career spanned from 1956 to 1969, was also a member of the NAACP while playing professional basketball, and supported the work of Dr. Martin Luther King Jr. At the same time, Russell encouraged fans and reporters to consider the teachings of Malcolm X as well, using his platform with media members to suggest an open mind and equal rights for all Americans. In 2011, president Barack Obama would honor Russell with the Presidential Medal of Freedom.

During 13 NBA seasons, Russell won 11 NBA championships and five MVP awards. He did this during the same amount of basketball that stretched from LeBron's rookie season through his third championship in 2016. Russell was an All-Star 12 times, retiring in 1969, just as Richard Nixon was taking office as the

37th president of the United States. By the time Russell marched on Washington in August of 1963 with Dr. King in advancement of civil rights, he had won six NBA championships and four MVPs.

Malcom X was assassinated on February 21, 1965, the same day Russell's Celtics lost to Jerry West and the Los Angeles Lakers 129–114. Dr. Martin Luther King, Jr. was gunned down roughly five years after marching on Washington with the Boston Celtics center and NBA's most valuable player, while standing on the Lorraine Motel's second floor balcony. Russell's Celtics played Game 1 of the Eastern Conference Finals against Wilt Chamberlain and the Philadelphia 76ers the next night.

Martin Luther King and Malcolm X were African American civil rights leaders and American martyrs who the NBA's most recognizable star publicly endorsed over several different occasions to members of the national media. These leaders were publicly assassinated in Memphis, Tennessee, and New York City, as Russell packed large arenas across those same United States with the Celtics. He'd continue their fight for justice and equality for the rest of his life.

All-Time Leader

Could NBA All-Stars eventually play for 25 years, consistently? Legends who hung up their heavily endorsed sneakers recently like Kobe Bryant and Kevin Garnett logged 20 NBA seasons. Tim Duncan almost played for 20, too, as well as Kareem Abdul-Jabbar and others throughout NBA history. We might have even evolved to the point where we expect our current crop of perennial All-Stars like Carmelo Anthony, Chris Paul, Blake Griffin, James Harden, Russell Westbrook, Kevin Durant, Stephen Curry, Kyrie Irving, and Anthony Davis to each play around two decades of NBA basketball before they retire. But could that 82-game grind eventually extend for five more seasons at some point in the future? Could LeBron play 25 years of NBA basketball? Could Karl-Anthony Towns? It would require a career that lasted long enough for 20 All-Star appearances to even begin to total the Legacy Points needed to match Russell on the all-time Legacy Points Power Ranking list.

Nobody will ever win 11 championships in 13 NBA seasons. Nobody will ever win 11 championships in an NBA career again after Russell. But could his 181 Legacy Points be threatened in other ways? No, not seriously. But where

Russell does leave himself theoretically vulnerable over the next 50 years is by only appearing in 12 All-Star games. He only played 13 professional seasons, of course, but Kareem still made 19 All-Star teams, Kobe 18, and it's conceivable that someone eventually earns 20 trips, or even 21. If LeBron played in nine more All-Star games from the ages of 32 to 41, for example, he'd retire with 21 ASG appearances. But that's only 64 of the 181 Legacy Points needed to reach the top of this ranking.

Tim Duncan retired in 2016 at the age of 40 with 15 All-Star checks on his resume. With the way he takes care of his body and advances in exercise, health, and diet, maybe LeBron plays in 20 All-Star games. Or, maybe the generation of NBA All-Stars who are currently growing up with LeBron's kids start hanging 25-year NBA careers on the board in the 2030s and 40s—assuming anyone even wants to play that long? At that point—a hypothetical 25-year NBA career where you make 20 All-Star teams, maybe earns enough points to surpass Michael Jordan at 137. But it's highly unlikely anyone ever catches Russell at 181.

Blocking Shots

The NBA was exclusively white until the mid-20th century, and the prevailing thought in the sport at the time was that staying on your feet to play defense without jumping was the best way to defend an opposing shot. Defenders were taught to not jump, for fear of the offensive player dribbling around your spot for a layup. In 1950, Chuck Cooper became the first African American player drafted by an NBA team when the Celtics selected him with the 14th overall pick. He'd break the color barrier along with Nat "Sweetwater" Clifton and Earl Lloyd during the 1950–51 season. Bill Russell joined the Celtics to start his professional career five years later.

Despite his coach's requests to the contrary at first, Russell saw an advantage in leaving the floor defensively to block an opposing player's field goal attempt. Instead of standing firm in your place, with both feet planted securely on the hardwood floor in defense of a spot or position near the basket with your arms outstretched above your head, Russell leaped in the air to alter the trajectory of an opposing players shot—while elevating his 6–10 frame into the air for the first time. He dominated the League as a result, crushing the confidence of his competitors with every suffocating rejection.

Bill Russell jumped off the floor to defend not only one spot, but now the entire painted area with his lateral quickness and leaping ability. Nobody had ever seen anything like it before, and the towering, athletically gifted center swiftly shattered the psyche of his opposition, who shook feverously at the thought of pending doom while Russell patrolled the key. In response to his dominance, other basketball players started jumping on defense, too, as the game continued to trend toward the sky for the next several decades. The same man who was working to change our culture as a civil rights activist was also changing the face of basketball forever at the same time.

Segregation and Basketball Camps

In 1961, Bill Russell's Celtics made headlines by boycotting a game to highlight the injustice of a restaurant on the road who refused to seat the team's African American players for dinner. After civil rights leader Medgar Evers was later assassinated in Jackson, Mississippi, Russell flew down to the heavily segregated town in the deep South of the 1960s to lead that city's first integrated basketball camp in another grassroots effort to raise awareness for equality.

Over five decades later, Bill Russell would have his named attached to the NBA championship MVP trophy, reminding us all what it truly means to dare enough for change that inspires others to do the same. He was the very best at what he did for a very long time in the NBA. He was Boston, he was the NBA. Russell was the embodiment of the American ideal. He was Bill Russell, the greatest champion in the history of American professional sports.

Following the 2016 NBA championship, Bill Russell congratulated LeBron James on the floor at Oracle Arena. "You paved the way," James told him. Which Russell most certainly did—for everyone.

LeBron vs. Bill Russell

Legacy Power Rankings: 97 vs. 181
Russell:
- **MVP award: 5 (35)**
- **NBA championship: 11 (110)**
- **NBA All-Star: 12 (36)**

LEBRON JAMES VS. BILL RUSSELL

LeBron James is not expected to threaten the 181 Legacy Points that Bill Russell totaled during an illustrious and equally important Hall of Fame basketball career. From year No. 14 for LeBron moving forward, expect him to compete more directly with Michael Jordan's 137 Legacy Points in his quest to enter the GOAT conversation of players, unlike Russell, who never played during the three-point era of NBA basketball. If James does win one more MVP, he's certainly not winning eight more championships to match Russell in each of those two categories. Even if he is selected to 20 All-Star teams before retiring, the road to Russell is long. But fortunately for LeBron, he is not competing directly with the 181 Legacy Points that Russell offers as a barometer of his greatness.

NBA players did not jump on defense before Bill Russell started doing it during the 1950s. African American players were not allowed in the League, either, until Russell was enrolled at McClymonds High School in Oakland, California. The three-point line was not invented until 10 years after Russell retired. Basketball was a different game for Russell than it is for James, considering they played their first seasons in the NBA more than 50 years apart. The NBA would not exist as we know it today without Bill Russell, but it's played much differently now.

People might not have started jumping until much later in basketball history if not for Russell, and he dominated his sport as much as any player in his era. He is a king just as Kareem and Michael were after him. But Bill, respectfully, is not the Greatest Player in NBA history. Since his retirement, Michael Jordan—who entered the League three years after the NBA three-point line was instituted, as a ball-handling wing who attacked from the perimeter—was and currently is considered the GOAT. It's Jordan who James will always be measured against, while none will ever again compare to the legacy and greatness of Bill Russell.

Chapter 34

★ ★ ★

Civic Leadership

To announce the start of Black History Month on February 1, 2017, LeBron James received the NAACP Jackie Robinson Award at a special presentation during the Cavaliers matchup at home against the Minnesota Timberwolves. The NAACP Press Release sent out to NBA media members that morning included the following.

"For the first time in nearly 18 years, the prestigious NAACP Jackie Robinson Sports Award will be presented to LeBron James—one of America's most respected, talented and influential athletes. This award is presented to individuals in sports for their high achievement in athletics and contributions in the pursuit of social justice, civil rights, and community involvement....

"Throughout his career, James has made charitable efforts a priority, namely through the LeBron James Family Foundation (LJFF). Founded by James in 2004, the program strives to positively affect the lives of children and young adults through education and co-curricular educational initiatives. In 2011, the Foundation began working on the high school dropout crisis facing LeBron's hometown community and launched its "Wheels for Education" program, which has since expanded with the "Akron I PROMISE Network." These initiatives support inner-city students with the programs, support, and mentors they need all the way through graduation. In partnership with The University of Akron, James has guaranteed college educations for thousands of Akron Public School students that complete the Foundation's programs and meet certain academic and philanthropic criteria. Through these efforts, James has

used his influence to move an entire community to rally around the youth in Akron and help them achieve their dreams through education.

"Coupled with his success on the court, James' diverse business portfolio of innovative endorsements and authentic investments has established him as one of the most popular figures in the world. Adding to his off-the-court portfolio, James continues to increase his influence in the entertainment industry through his production company, SpringHill Entertainment. Named after the public housing complex where James grew up in Akron, Ohio, SpringHill Entertainment is an entertainment and content company that develops creative content across a variety of platforms including digital, documentary and feature films, and scripted and unscripted TV."

James went for 27 points, 12 assists, and eight rebounds against young Karl Anthony-Towns, Andrew Wiggins, and the Timberwolves while accepting the NAACP award that night. His Cleveland team beat Minnesota by 28 while improving their record to 33–15 in defense of the Cavaliers 2016 NBA championship.

ESPYs Award Show Statement

LeBron James appeared alongside NBA superstars Carmelo Anthony, Chris Paul, and Dwyane Wade at the 2016 ESPY Awards in Los Angeles. The showcase opened with James and his colleagues speaking out in support of racial justice, following numerous high-profile shootings nationally.

Chris Paul spoke first. "Generations ago, legends like Jesse Owens, Jackie Robinson, Muhammad Ali, John Carlos, and Tommie Smith, Kareem Abdul-Jabbar, Jim Brown, Billie Jean King, Arthur Ashe, and countless others, they set a model for what athletes should stand for. So we choose to follow in their footsteps."

"The system is broken," Carmelo Anthony said. "The problems are not new, the violence is not new, and the racial divide definitely is not new, but the urgency for change is definitely at an all-time high."

Dwyane Wade then added, "The racial profiling has to stop. The shoot-to-kill mentality has to stop. Not seeing the value of black and brown bodies has to stop. But also the retaliation has to stop. The endless gun violence in places like Chicago, Dallas, not to mention Orlando, it has to stop. Enough. Enough is enough."

Finally, James spoke. "Tonight we're honoring Muhammad Ali, the GOAT," he said. "But to do his legacy any justice, let's use this moment as a call to action to all professional athletes to educate ourselves, explore these issues, speak up, use our influence, and renounce all violence and, most importantly, go back to our communities, invest our time, our resources, help rebuild them, help strengthen them, help change them. We all have to do better."

We All Have To Do Better

On Sunday, October 9, 2016, the Forum Section of the *Cleveland Plain Dealer* featured an image of LeBron James on its cover. In white font displayed over the black backdrop above the fold, were the following words laid out on either side of James:

"In the matter of our endorsement for president of the United States of America… We agree with his choice: Hillary Clinton."

Days earlier, James joined Clinton on stage and addressed a crowd gathered at the presidential rally in Ohio in an attempt to get out the vote for Hillary. The reigning NBA champion and four-time League MVP offered a passionate speech for the former United States first lady, senator, and secretary of state. He brought teammate J.R. Smith and his daughter with him as he took the stage. This event followed his full-throated endorsement of the Democratic nominee in an article published by *Business Insider* on October 2.

An excerpt of this op-ed offered by James is as follows:

"I support Hillary because she will build on the legacy of my good friend, president Barack Obama. I believe in what President Obama has done for our country and support her commitment to continuing that legacy.

"Like my foundation, Hillary has always been a champion for children and their futures. For over 40 years, she's been working to improve public schools, expand access to health care, support children's hospitals, and so much more.

"She wants to make sure kids have access to a good education, no matter what zip code they live in. She'll rebuild schools that are falling apart and put more money into computer science. She'll make sure teachers are paid what they deserve so they can give everything to their students.

"She also has plans to make college a reality for more people in America, especially for those who can't afford it. My kids in Akron are proof of the hope and motivation

that come from knowing college can be in their future, no matter what obstacles they might be facing.

"Finally, we must address the violence, of every kind, the African American community is experiencing in our streets and seeing on our TVs. I believe rebuilding our communities by focusing on at-risk children is a significant part of the solution. However, I am not a politician, I don't know everything it will take finally to end the violence. But I do know we need a president who brings us together and keeps us unified.

"Policies and ideas that divide us more are not the solution. We must all stand together—no matter where we are from or the color of our skin. And Hillary is running on the message of hope and unity that we need."

LeBron James Family Foundation

The LeBron James Family Foundation is an example of LeBron's dedication to civic leadership that goes far beyond the stump speeches he's made on behalf of presidential candidates like Barack Obama and Hillary Clinton. The foundation's work reaches much deeper into the community, serving to support children on an individual level throughout their formative years. The LeBron James Family Foundation is the vehicle that he has used throughout his professional basketball career to also be that same champion for children and their futures that he said Hillary is.

During that presidential endorsement speech, James referenced his foundation. He described it as a mission to give kids in Akron the resources and opportunities they need to achieve their dreams and create a better life for themselves. At the time, there were over 1,000 students in the Wheels for Education and Akron I PROMISE programs, which are managed under the foundation's umbrella of civic service.

Unlike any active NBA player before him, LeBron has used his brand and his platform as a global icon to help send and pay for college tuition for thousands of underprivileged children. Regardless of politics, children—all children, regardless of color, nationality, race, gender, or creed—must remain a bipartisan focus for everyone, just as they continue to be for LeBron.

Speaking out against Gun Violence

LeBron James posted a picture on social media on March 23, 2012, of himself and his Miami Heat teammates. They were all wearing the same team-issued

December 8, 2014: LeBron wears a t-shirt to honor Eric Garner during warmups before a game against the Brooklyn Nets at Barclays Center. (Icon Sportswire via AP Images)

hooded sweatshirt, with all of their hoods up in remembrance of Trayvon Martin. The unarmed 17-year-old boy who was shot by George Zimmerman, who escaped justice, in part, by claiming that the innocent child who was eating Skittles at the time, "Looks like he's up to no good, or he's on drugs or something," as Zimmerman told a 911 dispatcher shortly before he pursued and shot Martin.

The devastating murder, and subsequent failure of our justice system to hold Zimmerman accountable for taking a life, was and still is, simply outrageous. It's painful to even think this still happens in America, but it did, and it does. And while it can never bring Trayvon Martin back, or heal the wounds of his family, the fact that people as prominent and influential as LeBron, Dwyane Wade, Chris Bosh, and the NBA champion Miami Heat were making this statement matters. The hashtags, #WeAreTrayvonMartin, #Hoodies, #Stereotyped and #WeWantJustice accompanied this picture and call for civil rights justice, and love for all of our neighbors regardless of race, religion, or gender.

The Legacy of Bill Russell's NBA

Bill Russell's Celtics boycotted an NBA game because a hotel restaurant wouldn't serve the African American players dinner in the 1960s. Kareem Abdul-Jabbar would continue that legacy of strong, educated, African American scholars and athletes who would challenge the status quo and racial discriminations after Russell paved the way for so many. Michael Jordan would come to represent a significant step forward for race relations in our country as well, in the sense that he was the "Babe Ruth" of his era. Jordan was a young, black millionaire, entrepreneur, businessman, movie star, and athlete. He'd inspire others who looked like him to dream more than ever before. LeBron would be one of those kids who Jordan inspired, and he continues to carry the NBA torch and tradition of equality forward, along with the help of many others around the League.

LeBron and business partner Maverick Carter also asked why Phil Jackson, for example, had to refer to young black men as "posses" in a heated debate that sparked during the election year. The term suggests an Old West, renegade cowboy type vibe. A group of bandits riding into a salon after stealing a herd of cattle, potentially, or a group of modern-day gangbangers from the inner city. Why do LeBron and his friends remind Jackson and old white men just like him of anything other than people, or friends, or business partners? James politely asked this question, and Phil hasn't offered a good answer yet. The great Stan Van Gundy, however, said this.

"I'm going to be perfectly honest here, I've used that word before, okay. And when that all came out I had to ask myself, have I ever used that word before with a white player, and the answer is no. So, I think, look, you have to be aware of the language and you have to be aware a little bit of your own biases if you're going to overcome them and so I took that seriously."

Following the election of Donald J. Trump, who despite losing the popular vote by a significant margin, won enough of the Electoral College to secure the presidency, James posted this on his official Instagram account (@KingJames).

"As I woke up today looking and searching for answers on what has happened this song hit it right on the head! If we continue the faith (as hard as it may be to do so) we will BE ALRIGHT!! Parents and leaders of our children please let them know they can still change the world for the better! Don't lose a bit of faith! They're our future and we must remain stronger than ever!

"Yes we all wanna lace up the boots, put on the hard hats and strike but that's not the answer. Love, genuine LOVE and FAITH will be the only thing that can get us through this. Minorities and Women in all please know that this isn't the end, it's just a very challenging obstacle that we will overcome!!

"The man above will never put something in our paths that we can't handle no matter how difficult it may feel/be! To all the youth out there I PROMISE I'll continue to lead u guys every single day without no hesitation!! Time to educate and even more mold my children into being the greatest model citizens they can become in life! They will continue the legacy beyond life! Lastly, Even if whos now in office doesn't, Know that I LOVE YOU."

He included a video clip from Kendrick Lamar's song "Alright" with the message posted on his @kingjames Instagram account. He had just over 27 million followers around the world at the time.

Chapter 35

★ ★ ★

LeBron James vs. Michael Jordan

Michael Jordan
Professional Career: 1983–1993, 1994–1998, 2001–2003
NBA: Chicago Bulls, Washington Wizards
Legacy Points: 137 (No. 2)

No player in NBA history totaled as many Legacy Points as Michael Jordan since the Chicago Bulls selected the 6'6" shooting guard from North Carolina with the No. 3 overall pick in the 1984 Draft. The 137 points rank Jordan behind only Kareem Abdul-Jabbar and Bill Russell, while also declaring MJ the single greatest player in NBA history during the three-point era of professional basketball. For this reason—and many others—the kid from Laney High who was cut from his varsity basketball team before eventually taking over the galaxy would retire in 1998 as a six-time champion and five-time MVP. They called MJ the GOAT. That's who he was, and that's what he'll always be to so many.

Kobe Bryant's 111 Legacy Points are the next highest total after Michael's, as the quest to capture the ghost of Jordans past continues to rage among the uber-elite. Ever since he burst onto the scene as a high school phenom in the mid-1990s, Bryant was open and honest in describing his chase for Jordan's legacy. He was competing with not just other NBA teams on a nightly basis for twenty seasons, but also pushing himself to the very brink of his abilities, using every ounce of strategy, skill, talent, energy, and effort to also pursue the GOAT. For Kobe, Kevin, LeBron James, and anyone else with bearings to chase such heights, Michael's greatness was all they knew.

Jordan broke into the national basketball imagination forever as an All-Star for the Chicago Bulls in 1985. Throughout the better part of his career, MJ completely dominated the NBA, winning three rings in a row on two separate occasions. The League, the game, the dream, it all belonged to Michael Jeffrey Jordan—the sport of basketball was his. He was always the best player on the court. Always the most clutch. He was always the toughest—most courageous. He was never afraid. We never saw him sweat, never saw him blink. Children sang songs about wanting to be like him in TV commercials, we laughed as he joked with Mars Blackmon, and ate popcorn while he helped Bugs Bunny save the universe. He drank Gatorade, wore Nikes, ate Big Macs, and revolutionized professional sports on his way to basketball immortality.

"On nights I perform like Mike," Christopher Wallace once proclaimed. "Anyone, Tyson, Jordan, Jackson, action—ridiculous." He offered this line on Puff Daddy and the Family's Billboard topping *No Way Out* album under the stage name Notorious BIG. The point BIG was making is that he is among the very best lyrical performers to ever live. He offers this particular analogy to describe that larger theme, in a song titled "Victory." In it, he references the greatest boxer (Mike Tyson), basketball player (Mike Jordan), and singer (Mike Jackson) of that era to similarly describe his rightful place among MCs. When you mention the best, you mention Mike.

Jordan won his first NBA championship for the Chicago Bulls in 1991. He'd complete an NBA three-peat two seasons later, before re-launching a three-year campaign of dominance once again from 1996–98. He was 21 when he entered the League from UNC and 22 when he played in his first All-Star game. Five years after first appearing among the NBA's best, Jordan captured a ring at age 27. He would win his third at 29, and fourth at 32. The sport's most devastating competitor would also win his first MVP in '91 and fifth seven years later. Even as a 40-year-old for the Washington Wizards, Jordan played in 82 games, averaging 20.0 points, 6.1 rebounds, and 3.8 assists in a League that will never retire his legacy.

Air Jordan

Nike's original signature sneaker designed for Michael Jordan, the Air Jordan I, was released to the masses in 1985. The shoes were designed by Peter Moore, Tinker Hatfield, and Bruce Kilgore. Sneaker heads quickly devoured the design, and the shoe culture that currently thrives in basketball circles all over the globe officially began with the release of the first Air Jordans. They were fashion forward and structurally advanced, while introduced to the world on the soles of a budding icon.

For the next dozen years of Michael's career, Nike released an updated Air Jordan on an annual basis. Jordan's shoe would be sold and worn all over the world, representing a fashion statement of greatness announced by the name that inspired it's ever-evolving design. The Jumpman logo would become a symbol of basketball invincibility, and it would help Jordan launch his own brand during the decades that followed the massive success of his signature Nike sneaker line. The Jordan Brand would later employ the next generation of basketball superstars, carving their own legacies in a game His Airness helped spread all over the globe.

At the conclusion of the Great Sneaker Wars of the early 2000s, LeBron would eventually turn down record-setting advances and endorsement dollars from Reebok and Adidas to accept an earth-shattering contract from Nike. As Kobe Bryant continued his engagement with Adidas, the basketball shoe brand and industry that Jordan created with his success as a pitchman and player would look to LeBron to write its next chapter. He'd cash an enormous check to sign with Nike Basketball soon after graduating from St. Vincent-St. Mary High School in Akron in large part because it was the best business decision he could make. But the other reason driving James to Nike was the fact that Michael Jordan *was* Nike—and Michael was simply the best.

Final All-Star Game

In European soccer, the best offensive player or captain will wear No. 10. The number is a badge, an honor, it's a title that professional athletes train in the off-season to one day accept on soccer's biggest stages. To take the field or pitch as the best player on your team, wearing a number that publicly acknowledges as much, and promptly helping said team to victory is what every footballer dreams of. And even though it was never officially declared, or incorporated as part of basketball pageantry, Jordan made the No. 23 the NBA equivalent to futbol's 10. The best player on your team wore No. 23. If you played organized basketball at any level, the player who wore No. 23 was the best one you had. Just think about your 1990s-era grade school team, it happened organically all over America.

No. 23 appeared in the NBA All-Star game as a member of the Chicago Bulls for the last time in 1998. He'd earn two more All-Star bids after that, finishing with a total of 14, while concluding his playing career with the Washington Wizards. But during his last trip with Chicago, he dished out eight assists, grabbed six rebounds, and matched his famous number in the scoring column with 23. Ten years earlier, Jordan scored 40 on the All-Star stage (and in years in between he'd score 30, 28, and 26 in the highly anticipated winter classic). He'd log 382 minutes of NBA All-Star action in 13 games, scoring 262 points while hoisting three MVP awards. In 1988, he'd win his first MVP for his extended effort during the regular season, averaging 35 points, 5.5 rebounds, 5.9 assists, and 3.2 steals. One season earlier, he scored a career-high 37 per night.

Final Chapter

Jordan won his final NBA championship in 1998 as his shot over Bryon Russell signaled the end of a Hall of Fame career. When he left Chicago, after eliminating John Stockton, Karl Malone, and the Utah Jazz for his sixth ring, Jordan had earned 131 Legacy Points. He'd tack six more on the ledger with two All-Star appearances in Washington to round out at 137. During MJ's final season with the Bulls, he earned a total of 20 Legacy Points, winning the NBA championship (10), MVP (7), and making the All-Star team in the same year. Those 20 points earned by Jordan are the most that any player could ever win in one season, and it would isolate Air Jordan among the very best while claiming GOAT.

Prior to winning his sixth ring, fifth MVP, and playing in his 12th All-Star game in 1998, Jordan had earned the same amount of Legacy Points as Kobe would later total at 111. His 20-point effort that season, followed by two more trips to the All-Star game, would add the 26 Legacy Points that currently separate Jordan from Bryant on the all-time list. We can expect LeBron will need at least one more 20-point season of his own in order to approach his inspiration and idol, Air Jordan.

LeBron vs. Michael Jordan

Legacy Power Rankings: 97 vs. 137
Jordan:

- **MVP award: 5 (35)**
- **NBA championship: 6 (60)**
- **NBA All-Star: 14 (42)**

LeBron James drew within 33 Legacy Points of Michael Jordan after leading Cleveland to its first professional sports championship in 52 years. His Cavs would roar back in triumphant fashion from a 3–1 deficit in the Finals to defeat the historically great Golden State Warriors, who had just eclipsed Jordan's Bulls from 1997 to secure the best regular season record in NBA history. James would need to raise at least two more titles in Cleveland to stake his claim for the GOAT, however, entering the 2018 season 40 points back of His Airness.

Jordan won four NBA championships before he turned 33 years old. Can James win three NBA titles from 32 to 40 like Mike did? Kobe tried and got to five, retiring at 38. MJ was 38 when he won his sixth ring, six years older than LeBron is today. Are James, Kyrie Irving, Kevin Love, Tyronn Lue, and the Cavaliers poised to win two or three championships? The answer will ultimately define the GOAT discussion for decades to come. The debate over who James beat compared to who Jordan beat may also factor into this final ruling. James beat the 73-win, defending NBA champion Golden State Warriors led by two-time MVP Stephen Curry. If he beats the Warriors again now with Steph and Kevin Durant? I'm not sure Jordan ever beat a team as good as those two.

James logged more NBA miles than Jordan by the time he won Ring No. 3. He had played in more NBA games as a result of bypassing a college option that Jordan used for three seasons to begin his professional career immediately out of high school. In our day and age of modern medicine, vegan diets and health conscious teachings, the yoga-disciplined James might be in better shape than Mike at a similar age from a physical standpoint. This, potentially, despite banging his knees for many more minutes than Jordan on professional hardwood. The longevity and ultimate strength of LeBron's ability to endure will prove critical in his quest for all-time supremacy. But expect him to do just enough to make the claim before he hangs up his Nikes for good.

Chapter 36

★ ★ ★

First Championship in Cleveland

There are 10 teams in NBA history who have overcome a 3–1 deficit to win a postseason series. Three of those teams overcame such odds to win an Eastern Conference championship. Nobody has ever overcome a 3–1 deficit to win the Western Conference, and no other NBA team—prior to the 2016 Cleveland Cavaliers—had ever overcome a 3–1 series lead in the NBA Finals to win a ring. But when LeBron James, Kyrie Irving, and the Cavs found themselves down two games heading into Game 5 against Stephen Curry, Klay Thompson, and the Golden State Warriors, Cleveland would make new history.

Games 5, 6, and 7 of the 2016 NBA Finals are the three best performances that LeBron has ever had in back-to-back-to-back games during his professional career. Games 5 and 6, or 6 and 7, could also be called his two best games in a row since entering the League in 2003. After 13 seasons in the Association, Olympic gold, All-Star games, MVPs, and highlights that will live forever, LeBron had done what no professional athlete had ever accomplished since Jim Brown in 1964. He delivered an NBA championship to Northeast Ohio—just like he said he would when he returned.

The Cavaliers went from trailing 3–1 to an all-time historic championship parade at the conclusion of the series less than two weeks later. Just when the critics were lining up to crown Stephen Curry the NBA's new king, LeBron reached back to suggest we all just take a moment to reconsider. He proved to be the best player on the planet when it mattered most, and he'll have statues erected commemorating his achievements on the shores of Lake Erie because of it. He had proven once and for all that the fight is never over until you're all out of punches, and Cleveland had plenty of punches to spare.

Coach Lue

Ever since his earliest professional experiences as a rookie for Cleveland Cavaliers coach and former NBA legend Paul Silas, LeBron has often expressed his desire to play for a head coach who was also a former NBA player. In an attempt to present this option to keep James from leaving Cleveland in 2010, Dan Gilbert fired Mike Brown for the first of two firings and hired former Showtime Lakers star and Eastern Conference Champion coach Byron Scott. But the coach whose team led by Jason Kidd reached the NBA Finals twice would never end up coaching LeBron.

Roughly a dozen years after breaking into the NBA under Coach Silas, LeBron would lead a team once again that was coached by a former NBA player. David Blatt was hired to coach an up-and-coming Cavs team building around Kyrie Irving with Dion Waiters and Tristan Thompson as supporting pieces. If LeBron did not return to Cleveland, Blatt still may be coaching Kyrie and the Cavs. But James did. And he and James never built the relationship required to win on the NBA biggest stage. In lead assistant Tyronn Lue, however the bond would be markedly different right out the gate.

Lue was hired to replace a head coach who won two games in the 2015 NBA Finals while missing two of his three best players. He was also replacing a coach in Blatt who helped the Cavaliers to the best record in the Eastern Conference roughly midway through the season before being fired. But David Griffin made the decision, and Gilbert was willing to eat salary on now the fifth coach who was terminated during the season well before his guaranteed contract expired since purchasing the team from Gordon Gund. They were right, too, because the Cavaliers would gel at just the right time under Lue. He earned the team's respect and was willing to hold LeBron James accountable. James, who played with Shaquille O'Neal—the same MVP who was leading the Los Angeles Lakers to NBA championships with his buddy Ty Lue coming off the bench—respected

The chase-down block. (AP Photo/Eric Risberg, File)

Lue. He also appreciated his insight, and offered the best postseason series of his career under Coach Lue's direction in the NBA Finals. If James plays for another coach before he retires in six or eight or 10 years, I would be surprised. This relationship appears to be the proper mix of accountability and open dialogue, customized to James' leadership style specifically.

Ty Lue was a well-respected player in NBA circles during a decade-plus in the League. He was a key rotation player in support of Shaq and Kobe Bryant, who went on to learn the NBA coaching trade from the great Doc Rivers. After serving as Rivers' top assistant with the Boston Celtics and Los Angeles Clippers, Lue joined the Cleveland coaching staff as the highest paid assistant in the NBA only a couple months before James announced his return. Griffin and Gilbert pegged Blatt as their guy up front, but as it turned out they would find their head coach for the next decade in the pride of Mexico, Missouri.

Coming Back From 3–1

LeBron James averaged 36.3 points during Games 5, 6, and 7 to close out two-time reining MVP Stephen Curry and the Golden State Warriors. He scored 41 points twice during that stretch, while also dishing out at least 11 assists twice, grabbing 16 rebounds in Game 5, and a 27-point, 11-rebound, 11-assist triple-double in Game 7 to win his franchise their first NBA championship ever. Below are the numbers during that final stretch along with the highest Warriors player in each of the three major categories.

Game 5: June 13 at Oracle Arena

LeBron: 41 points, 16 rebounds, seven assists, three steals, and three blocks on 53 percent shooting overall and 4-of-8 from three-point range. Klay Thompson led Golden State with 37 points; Andre Igoudala added 11 rebounds and six assists, while Curry finished with 25.

Game 6: June 16 at Quicken Loans Arena

LeBron: 41 points, 11 assists, eight rebounds, four steals, and three blocks on 59.3 percent shooting overall and 3-of-6 from three-point range. Curry scored 30 and Thompson added 25 for Golden State. Draymond Green also added 10 rebounds and six assists.

Game 7: June 19 at Oracle Arena

LeBron: 27 points, 11 assists, 11 rebounds, two steals, and three blocks. One of those was The Block from behind in transition on what appeared to be a sure-thing Iguodala layup. Kyrie Irving hit The Shot, Kevin Love got The Stop, and the Warriors fell at home in Game 7. Draymond led the home team with 32 points, 15 rebounds, and nine assists. Curry and Thompson made only 12-of-36 three-point attempts and the Cavaliers accomplished the unthinkable on basketball's biggest stage.

First Team in NBA Finals History to Win Down 3–1

The 3–1 jokes and memes may always commemorate this series on social media. It will always be a thing the Cavaliers fans say even after the Warriors won in 2017. Hopefully the two teams meet again in 2018 and maybe even again after that as Kyrie, Kevin, Klay, and Draymond continue to enter their primes alongside LeBron, KD, and Steph. But the 3–1 deficit jokes also do an unintentional disservice to what it truly meant to defeat this historically great team with the NBA championship in the balance.

The Golden State Warriors did not choke. They maybe offered LeBron just a bit too much bulletin board material, maybe talked their way out of the championship in some remote respects. But beyond that, on the court, the Cavaliers just went and took it from a historically great team. Now, does the 73-win accomplishment by the Warriors—showing up every night as NBA fans pay hard earned money completely focused on winning the game—get diminished since they didn't win the title? Of course. But we can't forget that this was the team that had just won the title—they won 73 games as defending champs. So they should get some credit for that. They won the title in 2015, and then answered the critics who said they only won because Kyrie and Kevin were out by dominating the next 82 games they played. Steph is a revolutionary player. He and Klay are one of the most special backcourts in NBA history. Draymond is an All-NBA big and that's before they added Kevin Durant. LeBron and the Cavs beat this team—this elite collection of basketball talent—coming back from a spot that nobody had ever won from before.

Draymond averaged 20 points and 12.5 rebounds in Games 6 and 7. Klay averaged 25 over the last three games of the series and Steph averaged 24 during that stretch. LeBron just played the best basketball of his career while Kyrie exploded to make his claim as the top point guard in the NBA, and the rest of the team made plays when they needed to in order to defeat an historically great championship team that never quit once in the series. Golden State was blitzed by LeBron and the Cavs in the final three games of the series. They probably talked a little bit more junk than they would if they could do it over. And they didn't make the last couple plays the Cavaliers made to win Game 7. But the Warriors are one of the best teams to ever lose an NBA Finals series in the history of basketball. Which makes LeBron and his Cavaliers' accomplishments in 2016 so much more than a meme can ever truly convey.

Legacy Points Standings

LeBron entered the 2016–17 season ranked No. 9 all-time on the Legacy Power Rankings list with 94 Legacy Points. By securing his 12th All-Star Game and third NBA championship, LeBron earned just enough points to move past Shaq (No. 10) with 92 Legacy Points. He had begun the season with 81 Legacy Points after losing the year before in the NBA Finals to the same Warriors team LeBron just defeated. In winning the title, James moved past Larry Bird and Wilt Chamberlain (87 Legacy Points each) for the first time. The list of players that James now trailed on the Legacy Points Power Rankings following his first title in Cleveland are as follows: Bob Cousy, Julius Erving, Magic Johnson, Tim Duncan, Kobe Bryant, Michael Jordan, Kareem Abdul-Jabbar, and Bill Russell.

LeBron James activated 15 Legacy Points in 2009 when he was named NBA MVP for the very first time. The Legacy Points he's earned on an annual basis throughout his career are highlighted below. After earning his 13th trip to the NBA All-Star Game in February of 2017, the Cleveland Cavaliers forward currently has 97 Legacy Points. His current position is good for No. 9 on the Legacy Points Power Rankings, roughly 14 points behind Kobe Bryant (111 Legacy Points) and 40 behind Michael Jordan (137 Legacy Points).

LeBron James Legacy Points Year-By-Year

LeBron James	MVP LPs	All-Star LPs	Ring LPs	TOTAL LPs
2003–04	0	0	0	0
2004–05	0	3	0	3
2005–06	0	3	0	3
2006–07	0	3	0	3
2007–08	0	3	0	3
2008–09	7	3	0	10
2009–10	7	3	0	10
2010–11	0	3	0	3
2011–12	7	3	10	20
2012–13	7	3	10	20
2013–14	0	3	0	3
2014–15	0	3	0	3
2015–16	0	3	10	13
2016–17	0	3	0	3
TOTALS	28	39	30	97

LBJ vs. NBA: Doing Everything to Win

LeBron James came under intense scrutiny as the 2017 All-Star game approached for comments he made questioning the Cavaliers commitment to winning at an ownership level. This led Charles Barkley to question LeBron's competitive nature on TNT, and a response from James to the broadcaster. Days later, Shaquille O'Neal would use the desk he shared with Chuck to vehemently defend his former teammate and fellow superstar. Kevin Garnett, during his Area 21 segment of the broadcast, summed up the conversation following the verbal jabs from NBA Hall of Famers as follows:

Kevin Garnett via TNT on the Barkley vs. James debate of 2017:

"I looked at this and am just glad that it's starting to move in a direction where they're starting to come together and talk about the situation. But, if I was giving LeBron some advice I'd basically say that LeBron is being viewed in a different light. I don't think we have a player now in our game—maybe Steph Curry, maybe KD would be close—but when we're speaking great. LB is set up really to challenge Kareem's scoring record. He is going to be considered one of the greatest to ever pick up this ball. One of the greatest who ever played this game. He's being critiqued from that perspective, nothing underneath that. He's not good, he's not great, he's what we call the elite. He is in the conversation with probably four others. Obviously he was reacting to what Chuck said, but I would always advise him to keep things internal. And the best way to ever shut a critique up is by your play. I would tell him to go out and score 70. Then I would look in the camera and swag on Chuck in the camera. That would be the advice I'd give him."

The criticisms that Barkley initially leveled at James were potentially misworded but technically personal attacks if you're reading the transcript verbatim. I'm not sure Chuck meant them to be personal. But what he was speaking from was a competitive, alpha-male mindset that he had as a Hall of Fame player and others of his generation shared. Chuck was basically saying that LeBron should just act like he's the greatest and he needs no help because he already has a solid roster and is the defending champion. There is a level of toughness that Barkley was inherently questioning, in response to James speaking out against ownership for failing to have a starting-caliber NBA point guard coming off the bench or an insurance big off the bench. Specifically, it would appear James is exclusively referencing Griffin and Gilbert's decision not to sign Matthew Dellavedova and Timofey Mozgov.

Maybe LeBron was essentially telling Barkley to stay out of a conversation he knew nothing about. Maybe Gilbert had a conversation with James prior to his return in 2014 where he said that he would spend as much money possible to provide James with the best possible players in Cleveland. Incorporating the luxury tax hit and payroll expenses, Gilbert bankrolled the highest payroll in the NBA as a billionaire business owner and one of the wealthiest men in America. Maybe James was thinking—you could have signed Delly, you could have signed Mozgov. It would be an astronomical luxury tax hit. The payroll would be hilariously high compared to other teams around the League. But the Cavaliers could've signed Dellavedova and Mozgov under NBA team rules and decided the value was not worth the cost. They signed two D-League players at minimum contracts instead. And maybe that's what LeBron was trying to say without directly saying during the great Chuckster Debate of 2017 about doing everything possible to win.

Big Three All-Stars

At the top of the Cavaliers roster, Dan Gilbert did employ three max players who all made the All-Star Team together in 2017. Kyrie Irving and LeBron James were voted in by the fans as Eastern Conference starters. Love was named as a reserve player by the coaches for his first All-Star appearance in three seasons with the Cavaliers. Love appeared much more comfortable playing alongside his ball-dominant Big Three teammates as the 2017 ASG approached than he had in seasons past. He was averaging 20 points and 11 rebounds per night heading into the contest. LeBron averaged 26, eight, and nine while Kyrie averaged 24 and six dimes from the point guard spot. The last time LeBron appeared on the All-Star stage with two other teammates occurred in 2014 with Dwyane Wade and Chris Bosh as members of the Miami Heat.

Chapter 37

★ ★ ★

NBA All-Time Lists

All-Time Scoring List: 8th

On February 1, 2017, LeBron James was ranked No. 8 on the NBA's All-Time Scoring List with 27,961 points. He trailed Shaquille O'Neal for the No. 7 spot by roughly 600 points. Simple math suggests that scoring 20 points per game for 30 games will get James past Shaq by 2018 at the latest. In order to get into a top five that reads: Wilt Chamberlain (31,419), Michael Jordan (32,292), Kobe Bryant (33,643), Karl Malone (36,928), and Kareem Abdul-Jabbar (38,387), James would need to score roughly 32,500 points depending on how many Dirk Nowitzki finishes with (Dirk is currently No. 6 and only other active player besides LeBron in the top 15). For James, who is currently at roughly 28,000, scoring 3,500 more points is equivalent to averaging 20 points per game for 225 more games. We also believe that James will finish as a top five all-time scorer by the time he retires.

All-Time Assists List: 14th

LeBron James entered February 2017 with 7,188 all-time assists. That total was good enough for No. 14 on the assists list, one spot ahead of Terry Porter, two spots ahead of Tim Hardaway and three spots in front of the man who invented the modern day assist, Bob Cousy. It is likely that James will pass Lenny Wilkens and Maurice Cheeks to move into the No. 12 spot all-time but after that it becomes difficult. At No. 11 is the great Rod Strickland who dished out roughly 8,000 assists.

If James were to account for 900 more assists from February 2017 until he retires, he'd get there in about two seasons. It would then require another 1,000 assists to pass Gary Payton for the No. 8 spot all-time, and 3,000 more after that to catch Jason Kidd in the No. 2 spot. But assuming five assists per game for five more seasons at 70 games per season, expect James to finish with around 9,050 assists. If he does that, he'll finish No. 8 all-time on the NBA assists list, directly behind Isiah Thomas, Oscar Robertson, and Magic Johnson. John Stockton holds the all-time mark of 15,806 assists, which most likely will never be broken.

All-Time Steals List: 21st

At the conclusion of the 2017 NBA Finals, LeBron James ranked No. 20 overall with 1,749 career steals. Heading into the 2017–18 campaign, James will trail Kevin Garnett with 1,859 career steals and Kobe Bryant with 1,944. But if LeBron averaged one steal per game for six more seasons after this year, he'd total around 400 more steals. Projecting James at roughly 400 more steals, he would find himself around the 2,162 steals number that Hakeem Olajuwon totaled for No. 8 overall on the all-time steals list.

Top 10 All-Time

It seems relatively likely that LeBron will conclude his NBA career ranked No. 5 all-time in scoring. It is also relatively likely that he'll finish No. 8 on the all-time assists list and No. 8 on the all-time steals list. At worst, I'm suggesting that James will finish ranked in the Top 10 for scoring, assists and steals all-time. He is also currently ranked No. 84 on the all-time rebounding list. If LeBron plays 450 more games after the 2017 Finals and averages 5.5 boards per game he'll collect roughly 2,500 more rebounds. That would give James around 10,000 rebounds for his career, which would rank him inside the top 40 all-time rebounding totals. Top 10 in all-time points, assists and steals and top 40 in rebounding.

February 1, 2017, All-Time Lists

The NBA Legend chapters included in this book are referenced in bold on each of the all-time scoring, rebounds and assists lists featured below. These lists were via NBA.com as of February 1, 2017. The NBA all-time steals and blocks lists are also included, however prior to the three-point era of NBA basketball their maintenance in terms of statistical tracking was not collectively emphasized as much as it has become today. Also, more on a 7'1" center who finished in the Top 5 spots all-time in two categories and will be included on the Top 50 all-time for scoring, rebounding, and assists for decades to come if not forever below.

NBA ALL-TIME SCORING LIST

1. **Kareem Abdul-Jabbar**
2. **Karl Malone**
3. **Kobe Bryant**
4. **Michael Jordan**
5. **Wilt Chamberlain**
6. Dirk Nowitzki
7. **Shaquille O'Neal**
8. *LeBron James*
9. **Moses Malone**
10. Elvin Hayes
11. **Hakeem Olajuwon**
12. Oscar Robertson
13. Dominique Wilkins
14. **Tim Duncan**
15. John Havlicek
16. Paul Pierce
17. **Kevin Garnett**
18. Alex English
19. Reggie Miller
20. Jerry West
21. Patrick Ewing

22. Ray Allen
23. Allen Iverson
24. Vince Carter
25. Charles Barkley
26. Carmelo Anthony
27. Robert Parish
28. Adrian Dantley
29. Elgin Baylor
30. Clyde Drexler
31. Gary Payton
32. Larry Bird
33. Hal Greer
34. Dwyane Wade
35. Walt Bellamy
36. Bob Pettit
37. David Robinson
38. George Gervin
39. Mitch Richmond
40. Tom Chambers
41. Antawn Jamison
42. Joe Johnson
43. John Stockton
44. Pau Gasol
45. Bernard King
46. Clifford Robinson
47. Walter Davis
48. Terry Cummings
49. Bob Lanier
50. Eddie Johnson

NBA ALL-TIME REBOUNDING LEADERS

1. Wilt Chamberlain
2. Bill Russell

3. Kareem Abdul-Jabbar

4. Elvin Hayes

5. Moses Malone

6. Tim Duncan

7. Karl Malone

8. Robert Parish

9. Kevin Garnett

10. Nate Thurmond

11. Walt Bellamy

12. Wes Unseld

13. Hakeem Olajuwon

14. Shaquille O'Neal

15. Buck Williams

16. Jerry Lucas

17. Bob Pettit

18. Charles Barkley

19. Dikembe Mutombo

20. Paul Silas

21. Charles Oakley

22. Dennis Rodman

23. Kevin Willis

24. Dwight Howard

25. Patrick Ewing

26. Elgin Baylor

27. Dolph Schayes

28. Bill Bridges

29. Jack Sikma

30. Dirk Nowitzki

31. David Robinson

32. Ben Wallace

33. Dave Cowens

34. Bill Laimbeer

35. Otis Thorpe

36. Pau Gasol

37. Shawn Marion
38. Johnny Kerr
39. Bob Lanier
40. Sam Lacey
41. Dave DeBusschere
42. Tyson Chandler
43. Zach Randolph
44. Marcus Camby
45. A.C. Green
46. Horace Grant
47. Bailey Howell
48. Vlade Divac
49. Artis Gilmore
50. Johnny Green

NBA ALL-TIME ASSISTS LEADERS

1. John Stockton
2. Jason Kidd
3. Steve Nash
4. Mark Jackson
5. **Magic Johnson**
6. Oscar Robertson
7. Isiah Thomas
8. Gary Payton
9. Andre Miller
10. Chris Paul
11. Rod Strickland
12. Maurice Cheeks
13. Lenny Wilkens
14. *LeBron James*
15. Terry Porter
16. Tim Hardaway
17. **Bob Cousy**

18. Guy Rodgers
19. Muggsy Bogues
20. Deron Williams
21. Kevin Johnson
22. Derek Harper
23. Tony Parker
24. Nate Archibald
25. Stephon Marbury
26. John Lucas
27. Reggie Theus
28. Norm Nixon
29. Kobe Bryant
30. Jerry West
31. Scottie Pippen
32. Clyde Drexler
33. John Havlicek
34. Baron Davis
35. Mookie Blaylock
36. Sam Cassell
37. Rajon Rondo
38. Avery Johnson
39. Nick Van Exel
40. Larry Bird
41. Kareem Abdul-Jabbar
42. Chauncey Billups
43. Michael Jordan
44. Allen Iverson
45. Mike Bibby
46. Dennis Johnson
47. Kevin Garnett
48. Dave Bing
49. Damon Stoudamire
50. Jason Terry

NBA ALL-TIME STEALS LEADERS

1. John Stockton
2. Jason Kidd
3. Michael Jordan
4. Gary Payton
5. Maurice Cheeks
6. Scottie Pippen
7. Clyde Drexler
8. Hakeem Olajuwon
9. Alvin Robertson
10. Karl Malone
11. Mookie Blaylock
12. Allen Iverson
13. Derek Harper
14. Kobe Bryant
15. Chris Paul
16. Isiah Thomas
17. Kevin Garnett
18. Shawn Marion
19. Paul Pierce
20. Magic Johnson
21. LeBron James
22. Ron Harper
23. Metta World Peace
24. Lafayette Lever
25. Charles Barkley
26. Gus Williams
27. Hersey Hawkins
28. Eddie Jones
29. Rod Strickland
30. Mark Jackson
31. Terry Porter
32. Doc Rivers

33. Larry Bird

34. Doug Christie

35. Andre Miller

36. Nate McMillan

37. Jason Terry

38. Jeff Hornacek

39. Chris Mullin

40. Baron Davis

41. Kendall Gill

42. Andre Iguodala

43. Julius Erving

44. Reggie Miller

45. Dwyane Wade

46. Dennis Johnson

47. Micheal Ray Richardson

48. Ray Allen

49. Jerome Kersey

50. Tim Hardaway

NBA All-Time Leader in Blocked Shots

Some blocked shot data exists during the latter half of Bill Russell and Wilt Chamberlain's careers. These small sample sizes along with live accounts suggest that Russell and Chamberlain may have averaged between 8–10 blocked shots per game over several NBA seasons. But the tracking, analyzing and certainty of this defensive basketball metric did not become collectively confirmed and fully integrated until the late 1970s and early 1980s. It is also a metric that can be considered as part of the three-point era of NBA basketball which also began around the same time. So with Russell and Chamberlain aside and most likely way far alone at the top, below are the all-time leaders in blocked shots with totals that can be completely confirmed.

1. **Hakeem Olajuwon**

2. Dikembe Mutombo

3. **Kareem Abdul-Jabbar**

4. Mark Eaton

5. **Tim Duncan**
6. David Robinson
7. Patrick Ewing
8. **Shaquille O'Neal**
9. Tree Rollins
10. Robert Parish
11. Alonzo Mourning
12. Marcus Camby
13. Ben Wallace
14. Shawn Bradley
15. Manute Bol
16. George Johnson
17. **Kevin Garnett**
18. Larry Nance
19. Theo Ratliff
20. Dwight Howard
21. Elton Brand
22. Pau Gasol
23. Jermaine O'Neal
24. Elvin Hayes
25. Artis Gilmore
26. **Moses Malone**
27. Josh Smith
28. Kevin McHale
29. Vlade Divac
30. Herb Williams
31. Elden Campbell
32. Benoit Benjamin
33. Samuel Dalembert
34. Wayne Cooper
35. Caldwell Jones
36. Alton Lister
37. Andrei Kirilenko
38. Rasheed Wallace

39. Hot Rod Williams
40. Mark West
41. Erick Dampier
42. Clifford Robinson
43. Serge Ibaka
44. Terry Tyler
45. Zydrunas Ilgauskas
46. **Julius Erving**
47. Greg Ostertag
48. Shawn Kemp
49. Tyson Chandler
50. Dale Davis

Even if you add Bill Russell and Wilt Chamberlain to the top of the all-time blocks list, Kareem Abdul-Jabbar is still Top 5 in points, rebounds and blocks. He is also No. 41 in all-time assists. That is a spectacular line on an NBA resume and I'm not sure if the next generation took the time to clearly read Kareem's CV. It's an impressive body of work for the actor who played a pilot in the movie *Airplane.*

Another impressive summary that I'm not sure we fully appreciate or even appreciated during his career is the numbers that The Big Ticket hung on the board. While blazing a path once pioneered successfully by the great Moses Malone, Garnett helped high school basketball players and their families cash in on generational wealth as soon as they were legally allowed to fight and die for our country as 18-year-old men. He also won an NBA championship, helped team-mates get better, and currently ranks in the Top 50 for points (No. 17), rebounds (No. 9), assists (No. 47), steals (No. 17), and blocks (No. 17).

LeBron James will most likely retire as a player ranked in the Top 10 in scoring, assists and steals. He is currently No. 8 in points, No. 14 in assists, and No. 21 in steals. If he can continue to stack chase-down blocks and collect rebounds, he has a chance to join Garnett on the Top 50 for each of the five major statistical categories. Jordan, meanwhile, is Top 5 all-time in scoring and steals. He is also on the Top 50 in assists (No. 43). Like James, Jordan is not in the Top 50 all-time for rebounds or blocks.

Chapter 38

★ ★ ★

LeBron James Stats Section

The LeBron James Statistical Section was compiled by legendary Case Western Reserve University football player Dave Wooley, who was also site statistician for StepienRules.com during the Christian Eyenga era. He compiled and presented the data tables and spreadsheets featured below these paragraphs, as well as highlighting some of LeBron's most mind-blowing statistical accomplishments.

LeBron James is the only player in NBA history to average as many as 27 points, seven rebounds and seven assists for an entire career.

Additionally, LeBron is one of only eight players (Michael Jordan, Oscar Robertson, Jerry West, Clyde Drexler, Larry Bird, Rick Barry, and Russell Westbrook) to average 20/5/5. Only James, Magic Johnson, and the Big O averaged seven rebounds per game and seven assists per game in their career. Other comparisons between LeBron and Michael are listed below.

- FG%: LeBron .499 (and climbing), Michael Jordan .497
- 3FG%: LeBron .340 (1415/4156), Michael .327 (581/1778)
- APG: LeBron 7.0, Michael 5.3

With James at seven assists per game, compared to Jordan at 5.3 assists, that difference of 1.7 would account for at least 3.4 points per game. This would put LeBron above Michael in terms of points responsible per game. Furthermore, the fact that LeBron assists so often on three-point shots would make this number even more valuable in terms of offensive scoring. LeBron's assists have generated 16,662 points overall, which breaks out to 7,200 assists = 2.314 points/assist.

LeBron's First 47 Triple-Doubles

LeBron James has totaled 47 triple-doubles through February 1, 2017. His first triple-double came in Game No. 37 of his second NBA season. He scored 27 points, grabbed 11 rebounds, and dished out 10 assists. The year, game, triple-double summary are highlighted below for each of the next 46 triple-doubles of LeBron's career. Throughout his first 47 triple-doubles, James averaged 28 points, 11.4 rebounds, and 11.4 assists.

	Year	Game	Pts	Reb	Ast
1	2	37	27	11	10
2	2	39	28	12	10
3	2	74	40	10	10
4	2	80	27	14	14
5	3	10	36	11	10
6	3	29	32	11	11
7	3	44	26	11	10
8	3	52	43	12	11
9	3	68	37	11	12
10	4	39	30	10	10
11	5	5	32	15	13
12	5	9	39	13	14
13	5	13	37	12	12
14	5	14	30	11	10
15	5	47	26	13	11
16	5	48	31	14	12
17	5	58	24	10	11
18	6	32	16	10	11
19	6	36	30	11	10
20	6	43	23	15	11
21	6	62	14	10	12

22	6	63	32	13	11
23	6	64	34	10	13
24	6	68	26	11	10
25	7	2	23	11	12
26	7	30	34	16	10
27	7	55	43	13	15
28	7	66	29	12	12
29	8	8	20	11	14
30	8	28	32	11	10
31	8	32	27	11	10
32	8	72	27	10	12
33	10	16	26	13	11
34	10	39	31	10	11
35	10	53	16	10	11
36	10	67	25	12	10
37	11	68	17	10	12
38	12	66	20	10	12
39	12	69	21	10	11
40	13	50	21	10	10
41	13	67	33	11	11
42	13	70	27	11	11
43	14	1	19	11	14
44	14	12	31	10	13
45	14	14	26	10	13
46	14	40	26	10	12
47	14	41	24	13	11
	47	**Total:**	**1,318**	**537**	**537**
		Avg:	**28**	**11.4**	**11.4**

Playoff Record of Statistical Brilliance

LeBron James has consistently littered the box score with statistical dominance during the postseason throughout his career. From a scoring standpoint, James went for a first round career high 45 points in 2006 with the Cleveland

Cavaliers during a Game 5 win over the Washington Wizards. He also went for a Conference Semifinals high of 49 points during a Game 4 victory at Brooklyn in 2014 as a member of the Miami Heat.

LeBron's Game-By-Game Playoff Stats for First Round and Conference Semis

1st Rnd					Semis				
Year	Points	Result	Opp	Game	Year	Points	Result	Opp	Game
2006	45	W	WAS	5	2014	49	W	at BKN	4
2006	41	W	at WAS	3	2009	47	W	at ATL	3
2010	40	W	CHI	2	2008	45	L	at BOS	7
2010	39	L	at CHI	3	2012	40	W	at IND	4
2009	38	W	DET	1	2015	38	W	CHI	5
2006	38	L	at WAS	4	2010	38	W	at BOS	3
2010	37	W	at CHI	4	2007	36	W	NJN	2
2009	36	W	at DET	4	2011	35	W	at BOS	4
2008	34	L	WAS	5	2011	35	W	BOS	2
2008	34	W	at WAS	4	2010	35	W	BOS	1
2014	32	W	CHA	2	2008	35	L	at BOS	5
2012	32	W	at NYK	3	2009	34	W	ATL	1
2012	32	W	NYK	1	2015	33	W	CHI	2
2008	32	W	WAS	1	2011	33	W	BOS	5
2006	32	W	at WAS	6	2012	32	W	IND	1
2006	32	W	WAS	1	2008	32	W	BOS	6
2015	31	W	at BOS	3	2006	32	L	DET	6
2014	31	W	at CHA	4	2006	32	W	at DET	5
2011	31	L	at PHI	4	2012	30	W	IND	5
2007	31	W	at WAS	4	2007	30	W	at NJN	4
2015	30	W	BOS	2	2006	30	L	at DET	2
2014	30	W	at CHA	3	2014	29	W	BKN	5
2013	30	W	at MIL	4	2014	28	L	at BKN	3
2008	30	W	WAS	2	2012	28	W	at IND	6
2007	30	W	at WAS	3	2012	28	L	IND	2
2012	29	W	NYK	5	2016	27	W	ATL	2
2011	29	W	PHI	2	2015	27	L	at CHI	3
2009	29	W	DET	2	2013	27	W	at CHI	4
2016	27	W	DET	2	2010	27	L	at BOS	6
2015	27	W	at BOS	4	2009	27	W	at ATL	4
2014	27	W	CHA	1	2009	27	W	ATL	2

Year	Pts	W/L	Opp	#
2013	27	W	MIL	1
2012	27	L	at NYK	4
2008	27	W	at WAS	6
2007	27	W	WAS	2
2006	26	L	WAS	2
2009	25	W	at DET	3
2011	24	W	at PHI	3
2010	24	W	CHI	1
2007	23	W	WAS	1
2016	22	W	at DET	4
2016	22	W	DET	1
2013	22	W	at MIL	3
2008	22	L	at WAS	3
2011	21	W	PHI	1
2016	20	W	at DET	3
2015	20	W	BOS	1
2013	19	W	MIL	2
2012	19	W	NYK	2
2010	19	W	CHI	5
2011	16	W	PHI	5

Year	Pts	W/L	Opp	#
2006	27	L	at DET	7
2016	25	W	ATL	1
2015	25	W	at CHI	4
2013	25	W	at CHI	3
2016	24	W	at ATL	3
2013	24	L	CHI	1
2010	24	L	BOS	2
2013	23	W	CHI	5
2007	23	W	at NJN	6
2014	22	W	BKN	2
2014	22	W	BKN	1
2012	22	L	at IND	3
2011	22	W	BOS	1
2010	22	L	at BOS	4
2006	22	W	DET	4
2006	22	L	at DET	1
2016	21	W	at ATL	4
2008	21	W	BOS	4
2008	21	W	BOS	3
2008	21	L	at BOS	2
2007	21	W	NJN	1
2006	21	W	DET	3
2007	20	L	NJN	5
2015	19	L	CHI	1
2013	19	W	CHI	2
2007	18	L	at NJN	3
2015	15	W	at CHI	6
2011	15	L	at BOS	3
2010	15	L	BOS	5
2008	12	L	at BOS	1

During the Eastern Conference Finals, LeBron's scoring high came in a Game 1 loss to Dwight Howard, Stan Van Gundy, and the Orlando Magic in 2009. James totaled 49 points in defeat that night but it wasn't enough. During a Game 1 loss to the Golden State Warriors in 2015, James scored an NBA Finals career high 44 points. His next two highest scoring outputs in the NBA Finals came during Games 5 and 6 of 2016 when LeBron led Cleveland back to the championship with 41 points in two straight games. Another noteworthy stat in the all-time great rivalry that will hopefully occur for a third-straight time in the 2017 Finals this season between LeBron's Cavaliers and Stephen Curry's Warriors is this: The six top scoring games in LeBron's NBA Finals history have come against the Golden State Warriors during their matchups with Cleveland in 2015 and 2016 as listed below on the chart to the right.

LeBron's Game-By-Game Playoff Stats for Conference and NBA Finals

Conference Finals					NBA Finals				
Year	Points	Result	Opp	Game	Year	Points	Result	Opp	Game
2009	49	L	ORL	1	2015	44	L	at GSW	1
2007	48	W	at DET	5	2016	41	W	GSW	6
2012	45	W	at BOS	6	2016	41	W	at GSW	5
2009	44	L	at ORL	4	2015	40	L	at GSW	5
2009	41	L	at ORL	3	2015	40	W	GSW	3
2015	37	W	ATL	3	2015	39	W	at GSW	2
2009	37	W	ORL	5	2013	37	W	SAS	7
2013	36	L	IND	2	2014	35	W	at SAS	2
2011	35	W	CHI	4	2013	33	W	at SAS	4
2009	35	W	ORL	2	2016	32	W	GSW	3
2012	34	L	at BOS	3	2015	32	L	GSW	6
2012	34	W	BOS	2	2013	32	W	SAS	6
2016	33	W	at TOR	6	2012	32	W	at OKC	2
2014	32	W	IND	4	2014	31	L	at SAS	5
2013	32	W	IND	7	2012	30	L	at OKC	1
2012	32	W	BOS	1	2012	29	W	OKC	3
2007	32	W	DET	3	2014	28	L	SAS	4
2015	31	W	at ATL	1	2016	27	W	at GSW	7
2012	31	W	BOS	7	2012	26	W	OKC	5
2015	30	W	at ATL	2	2012	26	W	OKC	4
2013	30	W	IND	5	2016	25	L	GSW	4
2013	30	W	IND	1	2014	25	L	at SAS	1
2012	30	L	BOS	5	2013	25	L	at SAS	5
2016	29	L	at TOR	4	2007	25	L	SAS	3
2013	29	L	at IND	6	2007	25	L	at SAS	2

2012	29	L	at BOS	4	2011	24	W	DAL	1
2011	29	W	at CHI	2	2007	24	L	SAS	4
2011	28	W	at CHI	5	2016	23	L	at GSW	1
2014	26	W	IND	3	2014	22	L	SAS	3
2014	25	W	IND	6	2011	21	L	DAL	6
2014	25	L	at IND	1	2015	20	L	GSW	4
2009	25	L	at ORL	6	2011	20	L	DAL	2
2007	25	W	DET	4	2016	19	L	at GSW	2
2016	24	L	at TOR	3	2013	18	L	SAS	1
2016	24	W	TOR	1	2013	17	W	SAS	2
2013	24	L	at IND	4	2011	17	L	at DAL	5
2016	23	W	TOR	5	2011	17	W	at DAL	3
2016	23	W	TOR	2	2013	15	L	at SAS	3
2015	23	W	ATL	4	2007	14	L	at SAS	1
2014	22	W	at IND	2	2011	8	L	at DAL	4
2013	22	W	at IND	3					
2011	22	W	CHI	3					
2007	20	W	DET	6					
2007	19	L	at DET	2					
2011	15	L	at CHI	1					
2007	10	L	at DET	1					
2014	7	L	at IND	5					

LBJ Awards, Records and Standings

Awards	W	L	PCT	Titles
MVP–9, ROOK–1, ROY–1	35	47	0.427	
AS, NBA–2, MVP–6, MIP–6	42	40	0.512	
AS, NBA–1, MVP–2, MIP–19	50	32	0.61	
AS, NBA–2, MVP–5	50	32	0.61	CONF
AS, NBA–1, MVP–4, MIP–18	45	37	0.549	
AS, NBA–1, MVP–1, DEF–1, DPOY–2	66	16	0.805	DIV
AS, NBA–1, MVP–1, DEF–1, DPOY–4	61	21	0.744	DIV
AS, NBA–1, MVP–3, DEF–1, DPOY–9	58	24	0.707	CONF, DIV
AS, NBA–1, MVP–1, DEF–1, DPOY–4	46	20	0.697	NBA, CONF, DIV

AS, NBA–1, MVP–1, DEF–1, DPOY–2	66	16	0.805	NBA, CONF, DIV
AS, NBA–1, MVP–2, DEF–2, DPOY–6, MIP–20	54	28	0.659	CONF, DIV
AS, NBA–1, MVP–3, DPOY–13	53	29	0.646	CONF, DIV
AS, NBA–1, MVP–3, DPOY–11	57	25	0.695	NBA, CONF, DIV
AS	33	15	0.688	
4-MVP	716	382	0.652	3-NBA
10-ALL NBA 1ST TEAM	492	294	0.626	7-CONFERENCE
5-ALL DEFENSE 1ST TEAM	224	88	0.718	8-DIVISION
13-ALL-STAR STARTER	51	27	0.652	
2-ALL NBA 2ND TEAM				
1-ALL DEFENSE 2ND TEAM				

Chapter 39

★ ★ ★

Chasing Jordan: Legacy Points Prediction

LeBron James passed Michael Jordan on the all-time playoff scoring list after eliminating the Boston Celtics in Game 5 of the Eastern Conference Finals. He paid tribute to his idol during his press conference following the game.

"I think, first of all, you know, I wear the number because of Mike," LeBron James said of Michael Jordan. "I think I fell in love with the game because of Mike, just seeing what he was able to accomplish. But I felt like Mike was so—you know, when you're growing up and you're seeing Michael Jordan, it's almost like a god. So I didn't ever believe I could be Mike. So I started to focus myself on other players and other people around my neighborhood, because I never thought you could get to a point where Mike was. So I think that helped shape my game. And I think the biggest thing for me, sitting here today after breaking the all-time scoring record in playoff history, is that I did it just being me."

LeBron James made his 13th All-Star Game in 2017. He had also won two MVPs with the Cleveland Cavaliers and two more with the Miami Heat by that time, securing three championship rings overall. This gave LeBron a total of 97

Legacy Points heading into the 2017 NBA playoffs (including the All-Star points from this most recent season). This would put James 40 Legacy Points behind Michael Jordan. In order to make a rightful claim to MJ's All-Time throne, James would need to earn at least 41 Legacy Points before retirement. But expect LeBron to accomplish specifically that and eventually become known as the single greatest player in NBA history after retirement.

Outlined below is the way LeBron can earn more Legacy Points than the 137 totaled by Jordan before retiring from NBA basketball.

Assuming James plays 20 NBA seasons (the same total as Kobe Bryant, and one shy Kevin Garnett) he would retire in 2023. Following the 2016–17 campaign, James would then have six more seasons as a pro. That is six more seasons assuming he only plays for 20 years in the NBA. Should LeBron want to hang on and try to play with his son one day? That's a topic for another decade. But for now, I'm suggesting LeBron surpasses Jordan in terms of most Legacy Points earned during the NBA three-point era by any one player before he retires. Those Legacy Points we are projecting James to earn are highlighted below.

LBJ Legacy Projections

- Career Duration: 20 seasons
- Retirement Date: Following 2022–23 season
- Total Seasons after 2017 NBA Finals: 6

During the next six seasons of LeBron's career—following the 2017 NBA Finals—he would need to accomplish the following after falling to Golden State in the 2017 Finals.

All-Star Appearances: 5 (18x All-Star)

LeBron would need to make the All-Star team in each of the next five seasons following the 2017 ASG. That would give James 18 All-Star Games for his career. Kobe Bryant, as an example, totaled 18 ASGs as well, while amassing 111 Legacy Points. Bryant's Legacy Points total is the second highest behind Jordan during the NBA three-point era (1979–present).

By appearing in five more All-Star Games for a total of 18 trips to the ASG, James would move from 97 to 112 Legacy Points. But that's assuming James can continue to be named to the All-Star Game every season except for one before retiring in 2023. Friend and contemporary Chris Paul, for example, just saw his decade-plus ASG streaks snapped in 2017. But if James can keep his going the 15 Legacy Points he could potentially earn will prove critical.

NBA championship rings: 2 (5x NBA Champion)

I think he gets two rings at minimum following the first title James won for Cleveland in 2016. So in the 2018, 2019, 2020, 2021, 2022, 2023 NBA Finals, I am suggesting that James is on the winning team twice. One of those two times he'll be the team's best player. The final time he may be the second or third best player, but still contribute in all facets of the game, averaging something close to 14, 10, and 10 during the regular season. But I'm saying he wins a total of five rings before retirement. Five All-Star Appearances (15 Legacy Points), two NBA championships (20 Legacy Points), and MVP No. 5 would give James 42 Legacy

LeBron celebrates with the Larry O'Brien championship and Bill Russell MVP trophies following the 93–89 victory against the Golden State Warriors in Game 7 of the NBA Finals at Oracle Arena. Mandatory Credit: (Cary Edmondson-USA TODAY Sports)

Points. That's five championships, five MVPs, 18 ASGs for LeBron to make the GOAT status claim in good faith. Jordan has six, five, and 14 ASGs.

LeBron played in the NBA Finals every season for a decade pretty much. Is he a better all-around player? Bigger, faster, stronger? Does he have the same killer instinct as Jordan? Are you allowed to develop that? Because in the beginning, no, LeBron did not have that killer instinct. But it doesn't get much more instinctual or much more killer than it does being the first team in NBA history to come back from 3–1 in the NBA Finals. One that also came back against a team that broke Michael Jordan's Chicago Bulls best record before ultimately falling to a LeBron led team that kept punching. Don't answer now, answer after he wins two more and is announcing his retirement to let me know what you think at that point.

Michael Jordan's Final Six Seasons (1995–98, 2002–03)

Michael Jordan was playing minor league baseball in 1994. From his rookie season in 1984, however, to the onset of his second retirement (final retirement from Bulls, would play for Wizards after this) in 1998, he was a member of the Chicago Bulls. From 2001–03, Jordan came down from the owner's box to play for the Washington Wizards. Jordan's final six seasons as referred to below include the following.

2003 Wizards (39 years old)

2002 Wizards (38 years old)

1998 Bulls (34 years old)

1997 Bulls (33 years old)

1996 Bulls (32 years old)

1995 Bulls (31 years old)

During the final six seasons of Michael Jordan's career, His Airiness accomplished the following.

3 NBA championships (1996–98 Bulls)

2 NBA MVP Awards (1996, 1998 Bulls)

5 All-Star Games (3 Bulls, 2 Wizards)

Jordan totaled 30 championship points, 14 MVP points, and 15 ASG points for a total of 59 Legacy Points earned during the final six seasons of his career. Similarly, when compared in terms of age, after spending time at North Carolina under Dean Smith in college, Jordan would win his fourth NBA championship at the age of 32 years old. If LeBron and the Cavs win the 2017 NBA championship, he will have won his fourth championship by the same age (32) as MJ was when he won his fourth. Now, of course, Jordan three-peated, so James wouldn't have much time to get from four to six championships. But he is in the conversation and consistently wins his conference so there's a good chance he'll get a few more cracks at it.

My overall projections for James are that he plays at least 20 seasons and wins five championships during that time. He leads his team to four of those championships, and is the second or at worst third best player on the fifth one. He makes five more All-Star appearances after 2017, and wins one more League MVP somehow. That would be 42 Legacy Points—edging Michael by two—to give LeBron the most Legacy Points ever earned by any player in the three-point era of NBA basketball.

★ ★ ★
Resources

Along with the articles, videos, books, albums and movies specifically referenced and cited throughout this book, the following three outlets provided statistical, biographical and video footage that was directly cited or quoted.

Basketball-Reference.com

Kevin Garnett: http://www.basketball-reference.com/players/g/garneke01.html

Hakeem Olajuwon: http://www.basketball-reference.com/players/o/olajuha01.html

Moses Malone: http://www.basketball-reference.com/players/m/malonmo01.html

Wilt Chamberlain: http://www.basketball-reference.com/players/c/chambwi01.html

Larry Bird: http://www.basketball-reference.com/players/b/birdla01.html

Shaquille O'Neal: http://www.basketball-reference.com/players/o/onealsh01.html

Bob Cousy: http://www.basketball-reference.com/players/c/cousybo01.html

Julius Erving: http://www.basketball-reference.com/players/e/ervinju01.html

Magic Johnson: http://www.basketball-reference.com/players/j/johnsma02.html

Tim Duncan: http://www.basketball-reference.com/players/d/duncati01.html

Kobe Bryant: http://www.basketball-reference.com/players/b/bryanko01.html

Kareem Abdul-Jabbar: http://www.basketball-reference.com/players/a/abdulka01.html

Bill Russell: http://www.basketball-reference.com/players/r/russebi01.html

Michael Jordan: http://www.basketball-reference.com/players/j/jordami01.html

LeBron James: http://www.basketball-reference.com/players/j/jamesle01.html

NBA.com

Kevin Garnett: http://www.nba.com/players/kevin/garnett/708

Hakeem Olajuwon: http://www.nba.com/history/players/olajuwon_bio.html

Moses Malone: http://www.nba.com/history/players/malonem_bio.html

Wilt Chamberlain: http://www.nba.com/history/players/chamberlain_bio.html

Larry Bird: http://www.nba.com/history/players/bird_bio.html

Shaquille O'Neal: http://www.nba.com/shaqretires/

Bob Cousy: http://www.nba.com/history/players/cousy_bio.html

Julius Erving: http://www.nba.com/history/players/erving_bio.html

Magic Johnson: http://www.nba.com/history/players/johnsonm_bio.html

Tim Duncan: http://www.nba.com/spurs/tim-duncan-career-retrospective/

Kobe Bryant: http://www.nba.com/kobe-tribute/

Kareem Abdul-Jabbar: http://www.nba.com/history/players/abduljabbar_bio.html

Bill Russell: http://www.nba.com/history/players/russell_bio.html

Michael Jordan: http://www.nba.com/history/players/jordan_bio.html

LeBron James: http://www.nba.com/players/lebron/james/2544

YouTube.com

Kevin Garnett High School Mix: https://www.youtube.com/watch?v=Rp_SzdYd2gs

Hakeem Olajuwon's Ultimate Dream Shake Mix: https://www.youtube.com /watch?v=9J-WJ5739Tg

Moses Malone Career Mixtape: https://www.youtube.com/watch?v=niA1HKj2OfQ

Wilt Chamberlain A Real Superman (WIP #6): https://www.youtube.com /watch?v=iwvdsi6gLl8

Larry Bird Greatest Moments: https://www.youtube.com/watch?v=Bdm9542H-_Y

Shaquille O'Neal Top 10 Plays of His Career: https://www.youtube.com /watch?v=MDSFPvmA75o

Bob Cousy First Man To Dazzle NBA: https://www.youtube.com /watch?v=5QCP6mMMH2Q

Julius Erving Fish That Saved Pittsburgh Trailer: https://www.youtube.com /watch?v=Wre9bkg9Mxw

Magic Johnson Top 10 Plays of His Career: https://www.youtube.com /watch?v=yrC5x3UEx5s

Tim Duncan and LeBron James All Access: https://www.youtube.com /watch?v=IGY6UamVRSU

Kobe Bryant on ESPN The Life: 2001 Adidas ABCD Camp with LeBron: https://www .youtube.com/watch?v=lu5D0okNnmw

RESOURCES

Kareem Abdul-Jabbar in *Airplane!*: https://www.youtube.com/watch?v=n2A194yTWoQ

Bill Russell w/Muhammad Ali, Martin Luther King Jr. & President Obama: https://www.youtube.com/watch?v=D1OC2A4WRag

Michael Jordan Top 50 All-Time Plays: https://www.youtube.com/watch?v=LAr6oAKieHk

LeBron James takes over Game 5: https://www.youtube.com/watch?v=d1Px-jPm_TU

Additional Sites

http://www.nba.com/cavaliers/news/roy_press_conference.html

https://www.instagram.com/p/BKuDg2vhNH8/?hl=en

http://www.espn.com/nba/playoffs2006/columns/story?id=2419196

http://www.espn.com/nba/story/_/id/17978625/lebron-james-cleveland-cavaliers-passes-hakeem-olajuwon-10th-nba-all-scoring-list

http://www.espn.com/nba/story/_/id/18322243/lebron-james-cleveland-cavaliers-passes-moses-malone-eighth-nba-all-scoring-list

http://www.espn.com/nba/recap?gameId=270531008

https://www.usatoday.com/story/sports/nba/2013/05/05/lebron-james-mvp-bill-russell-kareem-abdul-jabbar-karl-malone-moses-malone-bob-pettit/2136567/

http://www.cleveland.com/cavs/index.ssf/2009/05/lebron_james_to_be_named_nba_m.html

http://www.cleveland.com/cavs/index.ssf/2010/05/lebron_james_wins_second_most.html

http://www.cbssports.com/nba/news/lebron-james-wins-his-first-nba-title-as-the-heat-close-out-the-thunder-121-106/

http://www.nba.com/video/channels/nba_tv/2013/05/27/thoughts-on-dr-j-lebron-james.nba/

http://www.nba.com/2013/news/06/21/lebron-garners-second-championship.ap/

https://twitter.com/kingjames/status/752598999211782144

https://www.si.com/nba/2014/07/11/lebron-james-cleveland-cavaliers

http://www.espn.com/nba/story/_/id/14266468/lebron-james-truly-sad-kobe-bryant-retiring

http://www.cleveland.com/cavs/index.ssf/2017/05/lebron_james_goes_from_reading.html

https://www.boston.com/sports/boston-celtics/2016/06/20/lebron-james-bill-russell-moment

https://theundefeated.com/features/lebron-james-pays-tribute-to-michael-jordan-after-breaking-record/